ISBN 978-0-266-00698-5
PIBN 10963152

1 MONTH OF
FREE
READING

at

www.ForgottenBooks.com

By purchasing this book you are
eligible for one month membership to
ForgottenBooks.com, giving you
unlimited access to our entire
collection of over 1,000,000 titles via
our web site and mobile apps.

To claim your free month visit:
www.forgottenbooks.com/free963152

English
Français
Deutsche
Italiano
Español
Português

www.forgottenbooks.com

Mythology Photography **Fiction**
Fishing Christianity **Art** Cooking
Essays Buddhism Freemasonry
Medicine **Biology** Music **Ancient
Egypt** Evolution Carpentry Physics
Dance Geology **Mathematics** Fitness
Shakespeare **Folklore** Yoga Marketing
Confidence Immortality Biographies
Poetry **Psychology** Witchcraft
Electronics Chemistry History **Law**
Accounting **Philosophy** Anthropology
Alchemy Drama Quantum Mechanics
Atheism Sexual Health **Ancient History**
Entrepreneurship Languages Sport
Paleontology Needlework Islam
Metaphysics Investment Archaeology
Parenting Statistics Criminology
Motivational

Historic, archived document

Do not assume content reflects current
scientific knowledge, policies, or practices.

CROPS AND MARKETS

Published Weekly by the
United States Department of Agriculture

CERTIFICATE: By direction of the Secretary of Agriculture the matter contained herein is published as statistical information and is required for the proper transaction of the public business. Free distribution is limited to copies "necessary in the transaction of public business required by law." Subscription price $1 per year (foreign rate $2) payable in cash or money order to the Superintendent of Documents, Government Printing Office, Washington, D. C.

WASHINGTON, D. C.   JUNE 6, 1925   VOL. 3, No. 23

Index to this Issue

Review

The livestock market was erratic for both cattle and hogs during the week May 25–30. Receipts of hogs were increased but shippers were not active. The big packers operated at certain figures and could not be forced to make purchases at inflated prices. Long fed, heavy bullocks arrived in more than sufficient numbers, forcing prices down except for the very selected ones. Yearlings and light steers were not plentiful and thus net gains were registered. The country demand for stockers and feeders was very light. Grass-fed animals were more numerous but not sufficient to burden the market or greatly affect the cow and lower grade steer market. Fat lambs arrived in light shipments and prices advanced 75¢–$1.25. The Corn-Belt shipments of lambs showed improvement in quality. The Northwest spring lambs made their first appearance at Omaha, commanding $15.75.

The meat trade was dull in spite of light receipts for most all classes of fresh meats. The increased shipments of veal were absorbed without much loss due to a more firm demand. The spring lambs formed the greater part of the lamb receipts with the heavy lambs gradually disappearing. Pork shipments were curtailed and the various centers indicated much irregularity in the market for loins and other pork cuts.

Georgia peach movement was becoming active the last week of May. Early varieties were expected to be cleaned up by June 10 and Carmans to start moving about that date. Georgia Belles and Elbertas probably will be a relatively light crop this year, but Hileys are very promising. A large portion of the 1924 Georgia peach crop was not marketed because of poor market conditions. Only 13,500 cars were shipped, and from the lighter crop of the present season possibly 12,800 cars will be shipped. Georgia leads all other States in output of fresh peaches, although production in California is far greater. California cans and dries large quantities of this fruit. The total United States peach crop last year had a farm value of $66,-000,000. Apples and grapes were the only fruits having a

greater value at the farm. Under the increasing arrivals from Georgia, prices generally declined during the week May 25–30. Potatoes made unexpected advances and closed very strong. Chicago carlot market quoted sacked northern round whites as high as $2 per 100 pounds; southern Bliss Triumphs up to $4.50 per sack, and South Carolina Cobblers at top of $8.50 per barrel. Shipping points everywhere reported an active demand and much higher prices. Maine Green Mountains reached $1.20 per 100 pounds f. o. b. Aroostook County. Cantaloupe and strawberry supplies were rather limited. Berry prices tended upward, while cantaloupes were irregular. The Imperial Valley season for cantaloupes is just beginning to get into full swing.

Butter markets gained strength during the week, May 25–30. Storing began in a larger way, although the movement was not nearly equal to that of the same period last year. Reports indicate a material increase in production during May over May, 1924. Foreign markets were firm and higher.

The cheese markets maintained a fair degree of firmness. Although trading was generally slow, stocks were kept well cleared and prices were closely maintained. The opinion of some was that prices should be lower while others held that this year's total production would be lighter and consequently prices for the present season were not out of line with what should be expected.

The grain market was firm, May 25–29. New crop futures were sharply higher on unfavorable crop reports and cash prices made slight advances. May futures moved out quietly. Offerings of wheat and corn were liberal but were absorbed without difficulty.

The hay market was slightly easier, with receipts running slightly in excess of the limited demand. Pastures and meadows in many sections were in need of rain, and forage crops were progressing slowly in much of the North. Timothy averaged slightly easier while alfalfa and prairie were draggy.

Feed markets turned easier. While prices for spot stocks held about steady the deferred deliveries, especially the distant ones, were quoted at substantial discounts. Bran for July, August, and September shipment was offered $4–$5 under prompt shipment prices. The export demand for oil meals was fair but the domestic demand very poor. The corn feeds situation was about unchanged with hominy feed offerings exceeding the demand. Supplies were generally sufficient and the production of most feeds good.

Cotton prices fluctuated within narrow limits during the period May 25–29, with final quotations down about ¼¢ per lb. July future contracts on the New York Cotton Exchange closed at 22.98¢ as compared with 23.20¢ last week and 29.65¢ a year ago, and on the New Orleans Cotton Exchange and the Chicago Board of Trade they closed at 23.30¢ and 23.60¢, respectively, as compared with 23.49¢ and 23.65¢ the previous week.

Livestock - Meats - Wool

Cattle and Hog Markets Erratic

Hog values continued their erratic way during the week May 25–30. Receipts showed marked expansion and shipping demand was irregular. In fact, about the only dependable feature that the week's irregular trade evolved was the fact that big killers seemed willing to operate around $12–$12.25 levels on light butchers but balked the moment shippers and speculative interests hoisted the price to $13.

The fat cattle trade was also erratic. Too many heavy steers arrived and in the main these tended lower, although handpicking developed and choice heavy bullocks reached the highest prices so far this month. Yearlings and light steers sold dependably and scored the only net gains registered in the fat-steer contingent.

Grass-fed animals became more numerous in the stock and the lower stratum of the steer run, but the supply of common and medium steers which showed expansion at some of the "river" markets was not large enough to force the small supply of fat she-stock any lower.

The country sent in many heavy long-fed bullocks while the supply of finished yearlings was not broad enough to go around. As a result good to choice light heifers included in mixed yearling consignments were not discriminated against, mixed steers and heifers topped the market at Chicago at $11.60, a point also reached by strictly choice yearling steers. The country was apathetic toward stocker and feeder steers and, although the latter were in very light supply, clearance was a slow process even at the recent sharp decline, a spread of $6–$7.25 taking the bulk.

Fat lambs had a different story to tell. Loadings were the smallest in weeks and prices worked 75¢–$1.25 higher on new crop arrivals which constitute practically all of the supply. While much of the advance on foot was not reflected in the dressed market, choice California-spring lambs sold upward to $16.50 at Chicago and a $16–$16.25 market developed late in the week. The quality of Corn Belt new croppers showed improved dressing qualifications and the tops sold practically as high as best western coast offerings. The upturn at the midwestern markets did not extend east and big killers brought in "directs" from Buffalo, an unusual occurrence.

Aged sheep held steady, California and native ewes comprised the bulk. Heavy native ewes sold around $6 but light weight offerings went mostly at $7–$7.50. California yearlings reached $12 at Chicago, where wethers from what State sold upward to $10. Northwestern spring lambs have started to appear, a string of Idahos making $15.75 during the week at Omaha. Feeding lambs were scarce and confined to thin westerns. Prices reached $13.65 at Chicago during the week under review.

Load after load of Nebraska-fed steers arrived at Chicago to sell at $10.50–$11.25. Eleven dollars was the practical stopping point on heavy offerings, 1,400–1,500 lb. averages being most numerous at $10.40–$10.85. Medium weights reached $11.35 and long yearlings from that State $11.50. A preponderant supply of the cattle runs at all markets consisted of steers and a liberal percentage were 1,100–1,300 lb. offerings grading good mostly. These moved slowly, lacking stability. Yearlings, on the other hand, sold uniformly, all grades getting action.

A spread of $9–$11 took most fed steers while $7.50–$8.50 took those kinds showing grass. Texas grass steers sold at $6–$7 at Kansas City and St. Louis, fed Texas going at $8.50–$9.25. The average cost of beef steers a week earlier at Chicago was $9.87 as contrasted with $9.53 a year earlier. Two Kosher holidays late in the week had the effect of curtailing early shipping demand but a general holiday, Memorial Day, made a short week, infusing considerable stimulation into the week-end sessions.

Wool Imports at Three Ports

Imports of wool through the port of Philadelphia during the week May 25–30, 1925, amounted to 1,906,857 lbs. grease and 12,780 lbs. scoured, valued at $540,475; imports through the port of Boston amounted to 1,179,486 lbs. grease, valued at $520,593; and at New York the imports amounted to 726,708 lbs. grease and 37,893 lbs. scoured, valued at $368,444.

Receipts, Shipments, and Local Slaughter

Week May 25–30, 1925, with Comparisons

Market	Cattle and calves [1]			Hogs			Sheep		
	Re-ceipts	Ship-ments	Local slaugh-ter	Re-ceipts	Ship-ments	Local slaugh-ter	Re-ceipts	Ship-ments	Local slaugh-ter
Chicago [2]	70,879	12,853	58,026	142,190	44,752	97,488	51,480	4,452	46,728
Denver [2]	8,108	5,506	3,127	10,577	2,883	8,961	5,530	4,864	1,080
East St. Louis [2]	28,961	7,421	18,256	74,264	42,051	29,089	15,474	3,053	12,381
Fort Worth	22,512	6,509	14,233	4,481	89	3,602	8,078	4,596	3,270
Indianapolis	8,952	4,741	5,111	86,014	16,985	16,008	968	492	563
Kansas City	34,076	9,179	24,883	51,317	94,619	27,409	21,140	3,289	16,539
Oklahoma City [2]	5,697	935	5,141	3,885	385	4,172	187	22	216
Omaha	27,699	7,005	19,955	75,082	23,002	51,505	24,152	1,712	21,043
St. Joseph [2]	10,503	2,054	6,033	38,764	13,284	27,110	15,971	222	12,167
St. Paul [2]	26,828	4,543	21,527	61,626	15,112	47,379	1,223	172	1,052
Sioux City [2]	16,722	4,939	8,550	66,292	38,760	37,910	1,238	21	1,149
Wichita [2]	5,009	3,234	2,030	16,363	134	15,503	871		971
Total	261,146	69,020	189,874	581,415	217,908	306,196	144,009	23,086	118,555
Total May 18–23, 1925	271,435	81,922	188,217	500,038	197,353	292,187	193,927	43,157	154,157
Total May 26–31, 1924	301,196	118,468	173,384	586,035	195,430	383,737	152,459	43,731	110,730

[1] Movement of calves May 25–30, 1925: Receipts, 66,574; shipments, 7,451; local slaughter, 61,685.

[2] Week ending Friday, May 29.

Average Weight and Cost of Hogs

Week May 25–30, 1925, with Comparisons

[Computed on packer and shipper purchases]

	Chicago		East St. Louis		Fort Worth		Kansas City		Omaha		St. Paul	
	Wt.	Cost	Wt.	Cost	Wt.	Cost	Wt.	Cost	Wt.	Cost	Wt.	Cost
	Lbs.	Per 100 lbs.	Lbs.	Per 100 lbs.	Lbs.	Per 100 lbs.	Lbs.	Per 100 lbs.	Lbs.	Per 100 lbs.	Lbs.	Per 100 lbs.
Monday	237	$11.90	207	$11.99	215	$11.56	247	$11.56	255	$11.52	228	$11.45
Tuesday	235	11.85	205	11.90	225	11.46	225	11.55	250	11.58	222	11.50
Wednesday	247	11.90	205	12.18	205	11.62	236	11.74	247	11.74	228	11.50
Thursday	243	12.16	204	13.58	216	11.66	232	11.84	244	11.91	229	11.94
Friday	232	12.05	206	12.11	219	11.66	238	11.58	248	11.50	234	11.74
Saturday												
Average												
May 25–30, 1925	238	11.94	206	12.11	215	11.61	234	11.65	249	11.63	229	11.63
May 18–23, 1925	234	12.35	205	12.43	206	11.64	235	11.88	250	11.84	227	11.93
May 26–31, 1924	237	7.20	212	7.25	201	7.07	229	6.93	249	6.77	230	6.75

[1] Holiday.

Weights and Prices of Stocker and Feeder Steers at Chicago

Week May 25–30, 1925, with Comparisons

Weight range	Number of head			Per cent of total by weight ranges			Average weight (pounds)			Average price per 100 pounds		
	Week May 25–30, 1925	Week May 18–23, 1925	Week May 31–June, 1924	Week May 25–30, 1925	Week May 18–23, 1925	Week May 31–June, 1924	Week May 25–30, 1925	Week May 18–23, 1925	Week May 31–June, 1924	Week May 25–30, 1925	Week May 18–23, 1925	Week May 31–June, 1924
1,001 lbs. up			.202			1.0			1,155			$9.53
901–1,000 lbs.	55	69	149	5.1	6.5	9.2	929	935	940	56.45	7.07	7.97
801–900 lbs.	218	69	395	20.1	7.6	24.5	831	829	835	6.58	6.39	11.50
701–800 lbs.	.263	.908	.353	24.5	42.8	21.8	741	720	747	6.54	6.63	7.18
700 lbs. down	541	386	518	50.3	42.3	32.0	594	594	613	6.31	6.53	7.05
Total	1,075	912	1,615	100.0	100.0	100.0	.695	.703	795	6.47	6.68	7.65

Pork.—In general the pork market was uneven with New York, possessing a steady trade, while at Chicago after the opening session, prices moved downward until there resulted a loss of $1, and at Philadelphia where the same condition existed the resulting loss was $1–$2. In contrast the Boston market displayed more activity and closed at a $1–$2 upturn. Other pork cuts were steady to 50¢ higher at Boston, and steady at New York, while at Philadelphia the market witnessed a $2 loss.

Light Receipts Affect Meat Prices Little

Boston, New York, Philadelphia, and Chicago

The wholesale meat trade was rather featureless for the week May 25–29. The light receipts of most all classes had little effect on price inflation as this trade condition was counterbalanced by a slow, draggy hand-to-mouth trade. The receipts of steer beef, cows, and lamb were below normal, in contrast with heavier shipments of mutton and veal at all eastern points, while pork loins were in larger amounts at New York and below the average supply at Boston. The retarded shipments of live beef animals during the week was a controlling factor in helping to stabilize the dressed-beef market at the eastern and western meat centers. Larger shipments of both live and dressed veal to the livestock markets and meat centers had a tendency to lower prices, but a slightly better tone to the demand for dressed carcasses prevented much slipping in the prices. The market in general had some weakness at the closing, as at the eastern points the closing market was steady to lower on all classes with the exception of pork loins at Boston which were $1–$2 higher, and at New York the heavier loins were steady to $1 higher. Other pork cuts at Boston were 50¢ higher, steady at New York, and 50¢–$2 lower at Philadelphia. The Chicago pork loin trade was draggy and a slight feeling of weakness was noticeable during the fore part of the week, but after slight price revisions were made the market appeared to stabilize and a steady course was held.

Beef.—Steer beef on the eastern markets consisted of all grades with the better quality carcasses not very plentiful and quite a few extremely common kinds were offered. Bulk of steers at Chicago moved at a price range of $15.50–$17.50 while a few strictly top yearlings reached $18.50–$19. These same prices were also prevalent in New York for the yearling carcasses. The Boston market opened 50¢ lower than for the previous week and only in a small way were transactions made at figures above the quotations, while most of the sales were at the minimum figure. Increasing number of the plain and common type carcasses on the market had the effect of lowering the cow market and a somewhat less effect on the better grades of steer carcasses. Bulls registered no noticeable changes in supply or demand and the prices remained unchanged. At Boston the sales were mostly $10–$11 while at New York carlots of bolognas were $9–$9.25. Kosher chucks and plates indicated very little fluctuation, although the early advances generally disappeared at the close.

Veal.—The receipts were increased at the eastern markets and the advances of the fore part of the week were lost. At Chicago the supply was moderate and with a slightly better demand there finally resulted an increase of $1. The lower grades of veal failed to command this premium. Choice vealers reached $22 at New York while the best figure at Boston was $20.

Lamb.—The demand for lamb was very irregular but a short curtailment of receipts enabled the market to close without great loss. There was little firmness at the close in New York due to the holiday trade. Lamb of heavy weight and poor quality received little attention and was absorbed only at reduced prices. Spring lamb formed the larger part of the shipments and moved at a price range of $23–$30.

Mutton.—The mutton market at Chicago showed some firmness due to the light supply of both mutton and heavy lamb, while in the East the heavy lamb and yearling contingent forced prices down $1–$2. The lower grades of mutton were numerous on the eastern market but they received little attention from the buyers and generally closed with a loss of $1–$2

Chicago Wholesale Prices of Cured Pork and Pork Products [1].

Week of May 25–30, 1925, with Comparisons

[In dollars per 100 pounds]

Commodity	May 25–30, 1925	May 18–23, 1925	May 26–31, 1924	3-year average [2]
Hams No. 1, smoked, 14–16 lbs. average	26.75	26.75	21.75	25.58
Hams No. 2, smoked, 14–16 lbs. average	24.50	24.50	19.50	23.04
Picnics, smoked, 4–8 lbs. average	16.25	16.25	12.12	14.17
Bacon No. 1, 6–8 lbs. average	36.50	36.50	24.75	29.83
Bacon No. 2, 6–8 lbs. average	32.50	32.62	18.75	23.00
Bellies, dry salt, 14–16 lbs. average	21.50	21.75	12.38	14.00
Backs, dry salt, 14–16 lbs. average	16.50	16.62	10.88	11.42
Kettle-rendered lard, tierces	17.75	17.75	12.88	------
Pure lard, tierces	16.75	16.75	11.88	12.67
Lard substitutes, tierces	14.00	14.00	12.62	13.33

[1] Based on average prices to retailers.
[2] Based on average prices for the following weeks: May 29–June 3, 1922; May 28–June 2, 1923; May 26–31, 1924.

Average Wholesale Prices of Western Dressed Fresh Meats

Week of May 25–30, 1925, with Comparisons

[In dollars per 100 pounds]

Kind and grade	Chicago				New York			
	May 25–30, 1925	May 18–23, 1925	May 26–31, 1924	3-year average [1]	May 25–30, 1925	May 18–23, 1925	May 26–31, 1924	3-year average [1]
Beef and Veal								
Beef:								
Steer—								
Choice	17.35	18.05	18.50	17.00	17.00	17.50	17.81	17.02
Good	16.10	16.50	17.50	16.00	15.50	16.20	16.38	15.88
Medium	14.60	15.00	15.75	14.88	14.50	15.20	14.75	14.67
Common	11.50	12.00	13.00	13.17	12.50	13.00	13.56	13.19
Cow—								
Good	13.50	13.50	13.50	13.00	13.00	13.80	13.81	13.48
Medium	11.00	11.00	12.00	11.92	11.50	12.30	12.02	12.08
Common	8.00	8.00	10.00	10.58	10.75	11.50	11.50	11.04
Bull—								
Medium	8.75	8.75	------	------	------	------	10.75	[2] 10.25
Common	8.25	8.25	8.50	8.31	------	------	9.25	[2] 9.25
Veal:								
Choice	16.80	17.10	17.50	17.58	19.00	19.80	17.50	18.67
Good	15.50	15.50	16.50	15.92	17.00	17.60	15.69	16.23
Medium	13.50	13.50	14.00	14.08	15.00	15.20	13.75	14.08
Common	12.00	12.00	10.00	11.17	12.50	12.50	11.12	[2] 11.50
Fresh Pork Cuts								
Hams:								
12–16 lbs. average	21.00	21.50	16.50	20.00	24.00	24.00	17.00	21.17
Loins: [3]								
8–10 lbs. average	24.10	25.10	18.75	19.50	27.60	27.60	19.25	19.96
10–12 lbs. average	22.10	23.10	17.19	18.15	26.60	26.00	17.81	18.81
12–15 lbs. average	20.60	21.30	15.44	16.65	24.00	23.70	16.31	17.60
15–18 lbs. average	18.50	18.50	13.88	15.42	21.00	21.20	15.00	16.54
18–22 lbs. average	17.50	17.50	12.94	14.33	19.00	19.10	13.81	15.58
Shoulders:								
Skinned	15.60	16.20	10.19	11.69	17.30	17.10	11.25	12.79
Picnics—								
4–6 lbs. average	14.10	14.50	9.50	11.08	15.50	15.50	9.75	[2] 10.06
6–8 lbs. average	------	------	9.00	10.42	14.50	14.50	9.25	11.08
Butts:								
Boston style	20.10	20.10	13.88	14.04	19.40	19.00	14.00	14.63
Spare ribs	13.10	14.10	8.75	8.35	15.00	15.00	9.00	10.50
Lamb and Mutton								
Lamb:								
Choice	24.50	25.50	28.50	28.92	24.60	25.10	29.25	28.79
Good	22.90	23.40	27.50	27.42	22.40	23.70	27.50	26.75
Medium	21.00	21.50	25.50	25.92	19.90	21.70	26.00	25.17
Common	19.00	19.00	23.00	23.83	------	------	24.50	23.50
Spring lamb, good and choice	27.00	28.00	30.00	30.50	26.60	28.00	30.50	30.50
Mutton:								
Good	14.50	14.50	16.75	18.12	15.80	17.60	15.25	16.29
Medium	13.00	13.00	13.88	15.59	14.30	15.80	13.38	14.15
Common	11.00	11.00	10.00	11.87	12.60	14.00	11.50	11.85

[1] Based on average prices for the following weeks: May 29–June 3, 1922; May 28–June 2, 1923; May 26–31, 1924.
[2] 2-year average.
[3] Loins 12–14 lbs., 14–16 lbs., 16 lbs. and over changed to 12–15 lbs., 15–18 lbs., and 18–22 lbs. average Jan. 5, 1925.

Boston Wool Market Quotations

The activities on the Boston wool market were somewhat restricted, although the tone of the market was very good. Conditions had become more stabilized with more buyers making inquiries. Values were holding firm with some lots of fine wools reaching the upper quotation, although the mills were resisting advances in prices. Fine wools were in greater demand and a line of fine and fine medium scoured territory stock moved at $1.10. South American wools were in some demand but only at low prices.

	Grease basis, fleece [1]	Scoured basis	
		Fleece	Territory
	Per pound	*Per pound*	*Per pound*
Fine strictly combing	$0.48–$0.49	$1.22–$1.28	$1.25–$1.30
Fine French combing	------	1.15–1.20	1.20–1.25
Fine clothing	.43–.44	1.12–1.15	1.15–1.20
½ blood strictly combing	.47–.48	1.13–1.18	1.15–1.20
½ blood clothing	.40–.42	1.00–1.05	1.02–1.07
⅜ blood strictly combing	.45–.46	.90–.95	.95–1.00
⅜ blood clothing	------	------	.90
¼ blood strictly combing	.42–.43	.85–.88	.85–.90
¼ blood clothing	------	------	.85
Low ¼ blood strictly combing	.40–.41	.75–.80	.75–.80
Common and braid	.38–.40	.65–.70	.65–.70

[1] The better class of Michigan, New York, Wisconsin and, Missouri wool 1–2¢ less. Kentucky and similar wool 2–5¢ higher depending on the particular lot offered. The above quotations depend to some extent on the individual lots.

Average Prices of Livestock, Week of May 25–30, 1925, With Comparisons

[In dollars per 100 pounds]

Kind and grade [1]	Chicago				East St. Louis				Fort Worth		Kansas City				Omaha				South St. Paul			
	May 25–30, 1925	May 18–23, 1925	May 26–31, 1924	3-year average [2]	May 25–30, 1925	May 18–23, 1925	May 26–31, 1924	3-year average [2]	May 25–30, 1925	May 26–31, 1924	May 25–30, 1925	May 18–23, 1925	May 26–31, 1924	3-year average [2]	May 25–30, 1925	May 18–23, 1925	May 26–31, 1924	3-year average [2]	May 25–30, 1925	May 18–23, 1925	May 26–31, 1924	3-year average [2]
Cattle																						
Slaughter cattle and calves:																						
Steers (1,100 lbs. up)—																						
Choice and prime	11.10	11.14	11.29	10.37	11.00	11.00	11.41	10.32	-----	-----	10.55	10.59	10.96	10.11	10.56	10.58	10.89	9.93	-----	-----	-----	-----
Good	10.51	10.55	10.44	9.67	10.12	10.16	10.53	9.73	-----	-----	9.60	9.64	9.93	9.41	9.57	9.60	9.89	9.26	9.42	9.46	10.05	9.18
Medium	9.48	9.50	9.18	8.83	9.34	9.42	9.00	8.74	7.50	7.45	8.70	8.77	8.55	8.54	8.76	8.84	8.58	8.40	8.30	8.30	8.35	8.13
Common	7.92	8.06	7.78	7.85	7.50	7.09	7.12	7.26	6.12	5.80	7.15	7.29	7.00	7.44	7.28	7.38	7.12	7.40	7.05	7.05	6.92	7.12
Steers (1,100 lbs. down)—																						
Choice and prime	11.56	11.58	10.81	10.22	11.25	11.25	11.19	10.21	-----	-----	10.94	10.98	10.62	9.95	10.84	10.86	10.68	9.86	-----	-----	-----	-----
Good	10.82	10.84	10.12	9.55	10.50	10.50	10.28	9.58	8.50	8.55	9.92	9.90	9.53	9.22	9.98	10.02	9.74	9.17	9.62	9.62	9.88	9.21
Medium	9.42	9.42	8.91	8.70	9.34	9.42	8.75	8.58	7.38	7.22	8.85	8.92	8.36	8.34	8.95	9.08	8.48	8.25	8.50	8.50	8.12	8.09
Common	7.76	7.91	7.22	7.57	7.38	7.56	6.75	7.03	5.88	5.60	6.92	7.05	6.75	7.17	7.09	7.20	6.81	7.06	6.92	6.92	6.50	6.93
Canner and cutter	6.25	6.25	5.25	5.19	5.38	5.52	4.72	4.33	4.25	3.68	4.92	5.04	4.62	4.33	5.21	5.26	4.84	[3] 4.54	5.12	5.12	4.62	4.12
Light yearling steers and heifers—																						
Good and prime (800 lbs. down) [4]	10.72	10.62	9.76	-----	10.62	10.62	9.53	-----	8.92	8.10	10.32	10.20	9.31	-----	10.05	10.02	9.56	-----	10.12	10.12	9.25	-----
Heifers—																						
Good and choice (850 lbs. up)	9.90	9.87	8.67	[3,5] 7.58	9.38	9.38	7.81	[3,5] 7.89	7.50	6.38	9.02	9.14	7.88	[3,5] 6.96	9.25	9.31	8.40	[3,5] 6.90	8.62	8.62	8.18	[3,5] 6.85
Common and medium (all weights)	7.42	7.38	6.34		6.88	7.02	5.84		5.00	4.00	6.50	6.58	5.12		6.59	6.70	6.00		6.12	6.12	6.18	
Cows—																						
Good and choice	7.40	7.40	7.32	[3,5] 6.03	7.08	7.28	6.91	[3,5] 5.66	5.70	5.38	6.88	7.02	6.91	[3,5] 5.64	6.92	7.18	7.09	[3,5] 6.06	6.88	6.92	6.60	[3,5] 5.64
Common and medium	5.31	5.36	5.26		5.38	5.60	5.09		3.95	3.80	5.05	5.10	4.85		5.02	5.20	5.07		5.12	5.12	4.68	
Canner and cutter	3.62	3.77	3.48	3.64	3.50	3.55	3.25	3.15	2.38	2.28	3.50	3.53	3.09	3.33	3.50	3.52	3.13	3.68	3.35	3.25	2.62	3.03
Bulls—																						
Good and choice (beef yearlings excluded)	6.51	6.62	6.16	[3,5] 5.70	6.25	6.25	6.25	[3,5] 5.37	4.38	4.12	6.04	6.18	5.30	[3,5] 4.99	6.06	6.25	5.75	[3,5] 5.39	5.60	5.62	5.38	[3,5] 5.06
Canner to medium (canner and bologna)	5.02	5.24	4.49		4.28	4.35	4.25		3.25	2.75	4.50	4.60	3.92		4.22	4.32	4.25		4.27	4.31	3.95	
Calves—																						
Medium to choice (190 lbs. down)	9.80	9.38	8.97	[3,6] 9.40	8.70	8.52	8.25	[3,6] 8.16	8.20	7.62	8.08	7.88	8.47	[3,6] 8.02	8.50	9.00	8.38	[3,6] 8.79	8.10	7.85	6.75	[3,6] 6.76
Medium to choice (190–260 lbs.)	8.60	8.40	7.62		7.70	7.00	7.31		6.90	6.80	6.95	6.75	7.47		7.12	7.50	7.31		7.00	7.18	5.98	
Medium to choice (260 lbs. up)	6.85	6.20	6.50	[7] 6.48	6.75	6.75	6.59	[7] 6.55	6.38	6.20	6.45	6.25	6.69	[7] 6.76	6.62	7.12	6.62	[7] 6.53	6.00	6.00	4.80	[7] 4.89
Cull and common (190 lbs. down) [4]	6.55	6.30	6.28	-----	5.25	5.25	5.25	-----	5.40	4.45	5.45	5.25	5.09	-----	5.62	5.88	5.56	-----	5.25	5.20	4.25	-----
Cull and common (190 lbs. up) [4]	5.35	5.25	5.56	-----	4.25	4.25	4.00	-----	4.12	3.70	4.25	4.25	4.09	-----	4.38	4.50	4.91	-----	4.00	4.00	4.00	-----
Feeder and stocker cattle and calves:																						
Steers—																						
Common to choice (750 lbs. up) [8]	7.00	7.38	8.19	7.60	6.65	6.75	6.75	6.76	6.12	5.98	6.82	6.85	7.22	7.39	6.77	7.03	7.41	7.17	6.68	6.75	7.10	6.51
Common to choice (750 lbs. down) [9]	6.88	7.02	7.09	6.91	6.52	6.62	6.44	6.07	5.88	5.48	6.75	6.78	6.22	6.53	6.62	6.94	6.59	6.58	6.42	6.50	6.55	6.10
Inferior (all weights) [4]	5.12	5.30	4.94	-----	4.40	4.50	4.28	-----	3.88	3.25	4.50	4.52	3.75	-----	4.62	4.80	4.11	-----	4.48	4.50	4.00	-----
Cows and heifers, common-choice	5.12	5.12	4.50	4.92	4.70	4.88	4.22	4.53	-----	3.62	5.10	5.32	4.47	4.70	4.88	4.95	4.72	4.95	4.32	4.38	4.12	4.36
Calves, common-choice [10]	-----	-----	-----	-----	-----	-----	-----	-----	-----	4.88	6.00	6.12	5.75	6.41	6.00	6.08	5.78	6.40	5.38	5.38	5.12	-----
Hogs																						
Top (highest price not average)	12.80	13.00	7.50	10.80	13.00	13.10	7.50	10.85	12.25	7.70	12.30	12.45	7.30	10.55	12.25	12.50	7.05	10.50	12.15	12.35	7.00	10.35
Bulk of sales	12.06	12.40	7.18	8.22	12.20	12.58	7.30	8.38	11.74	7.22	11.67	11.94	6.96	8.07	11.66	11.96	6.80	7.88	11.73	12.05	6.82	7.77
Heavy weight (250–350 lbs.) medium-choice	12.02	12.34	7.38	8.30	12.02	12.40	7.35	8.33	11.62	7.13	11.62	11.89	7.06	8.09	11.59	11.92	6.91	7.91	11.66	11.95	6.84	7.73
Medium weight (200–250 lbs.) medium-choice	12.14	12.48	7.30	8.37	12.16	12.52	7.38	8.40	11.66	7.23	11.71	12.00	7.04	8.15	11.70	11.96	6.82	7.94	11.68	12.00	6.82	7.81
Light weight (160–200 lbs.) common-choice	12.12	12.46	7.06	8.32	12.18	12.52	7.18	8.31	11.52	6.79	11.74	12.00	6.74	7.93	11.68	11.93	6.50	7.83	11.74	12.01	6.74	7.86
Light lights (130–160 lbs.) common-choice	11.82	12.22	6.44	7.93	12.03	12.28	6.60	7.90	10.66	6.60	11.62	11.73	6.28	7.65	11.51	11.78	6.25	-----	11.72	12.00	6.52	[3] 6.59
Packing hogs:																						
Smooth	10.98	11.23	6.68	7.51	10.57	10.76	6.41	7.11	10.25	6.38	10.80	11.00	6.51	7.16	10.90	11.33	6.41	7.24	10.37	10.73	6.25	7.00
Rough	10.58	10.92	6.53	7.23	10.22	10.40	6.25	6.88	9.50	5.88	10.58	10.75	6.38	7.00	10.64	11.08	6.23	7.00	10.12	10.48	6.16	6.67
Slaughter pigs (130 lbs. down) medium-choice	11.48	11.90	5.70	7.20	11.65	11.90	5.98	7.39	9.88	5.75	11.26	11.41	5.79	-----	11.12	11.10	4.92	-----	11.86	12.01	6.00	[3] 6.14
Feeder and stocker pigs (70–130 lbs.) common-choice	-----	-----	-----	-----	11.06	11.12	5.51	6.94	-----	-----	11.50	11.58	5.10	7.11	10.75	10.38	5.25	6.81	11.86	12.01	5.64	7.54
Sheep and lambs																						
Slaughter sheep and lambs: [11]																						
Lambs—																						
Light and handy weight (84 lbs. down), medium-prime	12.89	12.08	14.00	12.90	12.25	12.00	13.28	12.18	-----	-----	12.32	11.68	12.75	12.07	12.85	11.95	13.23	12.60	11.92	11.35	13.00	12.08
Heavy weight (92 lbs. up), medium-prime	11.88	11.08	-----	-----	10.95	10.70	-----	-----	-----	-----	-----	-----	-----	-----	11.58	10.88	-----	-----	10.88	10.18	-----	-----
All weights, cull and common	10.70	10.05	11.50	10.04	9.40	9.55	10.28	9.42	-----	-----	9.80	9.38	10.31	9.48	10.70	9.82	10.62	9.81	9.80	9.30	10.58	8.96
Spring lambs—																						
Medium to choice	15.30	14.70	15.48	14.79	14.48	14.32	15.38	14.30	-----	-----	14.50	13.55	14.71	13.78	14.92	14.32	15.56	14.67	14.35	14.15	14.50	-----
Cull and common	-----	-----	12.75	-----	-----	-----	12.00	-----	-----	-----	-----	-----	11.16	-----	-----	-----	12.62	-----	-----	-----	11.80	-----
Yearling wethers, medium-prime	10.75	10.12	11.62	10.47	9.55	9.30	10.88	9.74	-----	-----	10.05	9.72	10.25	9.71	9.75	8.95	10.62	9.94	9.75	9.12	10.65	0.73
Wethers (2 years old and over), medium-prime	8.25	8.12	8.12	7.30	7.50	7.60	7.38	6.80	8.00	5.88	7.65	7.72	6.56	6.47	7.60	7.50	7.41	7.23	7.48	7.50	7.15	6.67
Ewes, common-choice [4]	6.68	6.65	6.00	-----	5.75	5.80	5.50	-----	5.50	5.10	6.25	6.35	5.12	-----	6.38	6.38	5.59	-----	6.08	6.00	5.50	-----
Ewes, canner and cull [4]	3.32	3.30	2.88	-----	2.50	2.55	2.50	-----	3.00	2.70	3.00	3.10	2.38	-----	2.75	2.75	2.50	-----	2.62	2.62	2.38	-----

[1] Classification of livestock changed July 2, 1923.
[2] Based on average prices for the following weeks: May 29–June 3, 1922; May 28–June 2, 1923; May 26–31, 1924.
[3] 2-year average.
[4] No comparable grade in former classification.
[5] Old classification combined all grades; comparable figures are on that description.
[6] In old classification classed as light and medium weight.
[7] In old classification classed as heavy weight.
[8] Data previous to July, 1923, are averages of feeder steers, 1,000 and 750–1,000 lbs. in former classification.
[9] In old classification classed as stocker steers, common-choice.
[10] Data previous to July, 1923, are averages of stocker calves, good and choice and common and medium in former classification.
[11] Shorn basis.

Stocker and Feeder Shipments
Week May 23-29, 1925, with Comparisons

Origin and destination	Cattle and calves		Hogs		Sheep	
	Week May 23-29, 1925	Per cent of average of corresponding week 1922, 1923, 1924	Week May 23-29, 1925	Per cent of average of corresponding week 1922, 1923, 1924	Week May 23-29, 1925	Per cent of average of corresponding week 1922, 1923, 1924
Market origin:						
Chicago	1,867	80.5			1,843	44.9
Denver	4,237	51.0	2,885	213.7	930	64.4
East St. Louis	1,180	47.8			315	
Fort Worth	4,287	118.0	164	4.26	898	135.0
Indianapolis	538	73.6	109	35.1	15	16.3
Kansas City	4,271	37.6	833	35.5	2,963	67.1
Oklahoma City	129	14.8				
Omaha	2,438	60.9			755	20.6
St. Joseph	600	87.2	217	107.4	450	26.2
St. Paul	3,314	89.2	4,086	136.1	9	7.8
Sioux City	2,646	71.4	921		21	77.8
Wichita	2,370	94.8	134	73.2		
Total	27,886	62.4	9,379	92.8	8,199	54.0
State destination:						
California			2,283	278.4		
Colorado	2,689	110.4	380	83.9	827	83.7
Illinois	2,453	63.3	443	47.4	589	61.3
Indiana	1,026	77.9	706	100.4	805	108.8
Iowa	3,002	41.2	1,161	38.3	368	32.7
Kansas	4,387	71.3	179	98.4	239	26.9
Kentucky	144	90.0				
Michigan	1,192	252.5	382	111.0	883	34.6
Minnesota	922	145.4	1,928	186.8	265	83.6
Missouri	2,139	58.3	209	26.6	2,139	62.5
Montana	22	36.1				
Nebraska	4,154	63.4	641	134.7	804	24.0
New Jersey			454			
New Mexico	19					
New York	88	18.8				
North Dakota	30	56.6				
Ohio	913	89.2	114	36.9	750	378.8
Oklahoma	963	66.0				
Pennsylvania	338	121.6				
South Dakota	905	32.4				
Texas	1,660	130.6	208	163.7	870	130.8
Virginia	43	74.1				
West Virginia			221			
Wisconsin	240	20.7				
Wyoming	587	28.1				
Total	27,886	62.4	9,379	92.8	8,199	54.0

Season Comparisons of Stocker and Feeder Shipments

	Cattle and calves	Hogs	Sheep
July 1, 1924, to May 29, 1925	3,040,223	330,913	3,288,394
Same period one year ago	3,672,470	550,254	3,253,740
Same period two years ago	3,942,907	557,045	2,018,786
Same period three years ago	3,030,343	338,628	2,348,047
Current period as per cent of average of three previous periods	85.7	68.2	115.8

Beef Steers Sold Out of First Hands for Slaughter at Chicago
Week May 25-30, 1925, with Comparisons

Grade	Number of head			Per cent of total by grades			Average weight (pounds)			Average price per 100 pounds		
	Week May 25-30, 1925	Week May 30, 1925	Week May 31, 1924	Week May 25-30, 1925	Week May 30, 1925	Week May 31, 1924	Week May 25-30, 1925	Week May 30, 1925	Week May 31, 1924	Week May 25-30, 1925	Week May 30, 1925	Week May 31, 1924
Choice and prime	4,663	3,436	1,180	17.8	13.5	5.2	1,297	1,357	1,304	$10.69	$10.64	$10.91
Good	7,416	7,715	5,734	28.4	30.3	25.3	1,136	1,134	1,154	10.36	10.36	10.10
Medium	12,557	12,573	13,682	48.0	49.4	60.3	987	992	978	9.55	9.46	8.97
Common	1,525	1,722	2,087	5.8	6.8	9.2	842	820	776	7.86	7.97	7.50
Total	26,161	25,446	22,683	100.0	100.0	100.0	1,070	1,073	1,021	9.96	9.87	9.32

Dairy and Poultry

Butter Markets Firm

During the week, May 25-30, butter markets were generally in a firm position and prices showed advances at all markets, the advances averaging about 1¢. While demand from consuming outlets was quite satisfactory, yet the firmness which persisted in spite of heavier receipts and some accumulation in trading stocks was in considerable part due to speculative interest on the Chicago and New York markets which, while not forcing further advances after the beginning of the week, served to hold the market level and prevent declines. Medium and undergrades were still in relatively short supply, indicating that quality of arrivals was very good. Centralized butter being scarcely adequate for the demand was somewhat firmer throughout the week than other types of butter.

The into-storage movement which had already begun during the preceding week was greatly accelerated and storage holdings at the four markets showed a net gain of slightly more than two million pounds. Thus, the storage season may be considered as well under way. Many prospective stores were reported as holding off until the first of the month in order to get the desirable June dates on their goods. Storing during the week under review was largely of two types, that of operators who were convinced that price levels were about as low as they could be expected to get, and that butter was a good speculative buy, and in equal amount to dealers who, finding themselves heavily stocked with high-cost butter which could not be sold at a profit, preferred to send such goods to storage. Considerable optimism regarding the prospects of this year's storage deal was expressed from many quarters. In spite of the heavy increase of the current week, storage holdings were considerably lighter than last year, and the prevailing belief was that production, which was heavier than in May, 1924, would not be sustained throughout June and July such as occurred last year and which accounted for the tremendous storage holdings of last season.

All indications are that production during May this year has run somewhat heavier than the same month in 1924. This is borne out by reports from various creameries and producing organizations which place the increase from 3 to 16%, the larger increase being reported from cooperative creamery territory. Receipts at the four markets were also heavier than during May, 1924. This increase is thought to be the result of the earlier season in most producing sections, this year the season being slightly advanced where last year it was slightly retarded. However, production since the first of January is still about 4% lighter than in 1924, which accounts for the higher prices prevailing at present. Production for the next few months is generally regarded as probably being lighter than last year, due to the lack of rain in important sections and the fact that herds were not fed sufficient concentrates during the winter months to insure sustained milk flow on grass.

The Copenhagen market showed a firmer trend and the official quotation was settled at 434 kroner. This is an advance of 12 kroner, which, when converted at the prevailing rate of exchange, is an advance of nearly 1 cent per pound. The Thursday quotation equaled 37.04 cents as compared with 36.11 cents a week previous. Canadian markets were reported as about steady with practically no changes in prices as established on the Montreal auctions. No imports of any note were reported during the week except for one car of Canadian butter received at New York. The firm development noted would seem to make further imports even less likely.

Cheese Markets Continue Steady

During the trading week, May 25-29, the cheese markets maintained fairly well the degree of firmness which has been evident for some time. At the opening of the week country prices were advanced fractionally in line with higher board rulings and for the most part the usual margins were in effect. Trading was generally slow, as most dealers reported rather light trading throughout the week. At times some irregularity in tone became apparent, but no real weakness developed, for, except on Longhorns, practically no accumulation of stock was noted. At the close there was slight reduction in the board prices established Friday, May 28, indicating that for the present a demand sufficient to clear receipts was the supporting factor.

Distributing markets, notably the larger ones, are still lacking the buying support which is being given country points both at Wisconsin and in New York State. At Chicago the tone was reported as no more than steady at anytime with an easy and unsettled undertone prevailing. Most buyers were taking only sufficient stocks to supply current needs and toward the end of the week buyers were asking for concessions. Practically all eastern markets were carrying light supplies of new cheese mostly owing to lack of confidence in the maintenance of levels at primary points. However, the demand was not brisk and generally speaking most sales were at prices which showed a very small margin of profit when replacement costs were considered.

The sentiment among many operators regarding storing at the present prices appeared distinctly unfavorable and there was very little buying for this purpose. However, the opinion was expressed by some observers that the prevailing level of prices may not be out of line for this season. They hold that production for this time of year is heavy as compared with last season and that there is reason to believe the flush period will be of shorter duration. Practically no activity now noted in wholesale channels on cured cheese. The remaining supplies are being steadily depleted and all prices are well maintained.

Dairy and Poultry Products at Five Markets

New York, Chicago, Philadelphia, Boston, and San Francisco

	Week ending May 30, 1925	Previous week	Last year
Butter:	*Pounds*	*Pounds*	*Pounds*
Receipts for week	16,693,226	18,219,490	16,995,174
Receipts since Jan. 1	256,929,700	240,236,474	268,554,373
Put into cold storage	2,830,359	1,812,073	3,234,748
Withdrawn from cold storage	554,130	363,425	507,990
Change during week	+2,276,229	+1,448,648	+2,726,758
Total holdings	5,471,771	3,195,542	10,937,456
Cheese:			
Receipts for week	4,308,981	4,568,642	4,249,938
Receipts since Jan. 1	76,641,343	72,332,362	81,734,935
Put into cold storage	1,191,094	1,176,144	1,140,243
Withdrawn from cold storage	1,004,826	1,228,264	925,791
Change during week	+186,268	−52,120	+214,452
Total holdings	12,418,733	12,232,465	10,014,060
Dressed Poultry:			
Receipts for week	4,524,580	3,689,582	4,282,074
Receipts since Jan. 1	96,938,876	92,414,296	118,975,971
Put into cold storage	2,114,031	1,420,858	1,780,832
Withdrawn from cold storage	3,657,813	3,935,941	2,996,678
Change during week	−1,543,782	−2,516,083	−1,215,846
Total holdings	48,243,841	49,787,023	28,135,300
Eggs:	*Cases*	*Cases*	*Cases*
Receipts for week	465,757	512,746	500,777
Receipts since Jan. 1	8,383,248	7,917,491	8,456,662
Put into cold storage	239,804	276,505	303,009
Withdrawn from cold storage	28,673	27,203	11,013
Change during week	+211,131	+249,302	+291,996
Total holdings	2,893,971	2,682,840	2,754,215

The Foreign Dairy Situation

At this time of the year the world supplies of dairy products are heaviest and prices are subject to the greatest seasonal decline. Under modern conditions markets in the deficit countries have two seasons of supply each year. These two periods of flush production tend to overlap in the spring months and to leave a gap in which supplies are lighter during several months of late summer and early autumn. Diminishing but still considerable shipments, especially of butter, are now reaching the markets of Europe from the south, while rapidly growing supplies are forthcoming in both the importing and exporting countries of the north.

Although butter production in Australia and New Zealand has declined seasonally to a fraction of the December and January output considerable quantities produced earlier in the season are still being received on European markets. Russian butter export authorities are making arrangements to export about 22,500,000 pounds principally to England and Germany. This is nearly double the amount exported last season.

Foreign markets continue strong enough to keep United States markets practically free of foreign supplies. A detailed report on the Foreign Dairy Situation for the month of April will be forwarded to anyone interested upon request to the Foreign Service, Bureau of Agricultural Economics, Washington, D. C., for Foreign Crops and Markets, vol. 10, No. 22.

Wholesale Prices of Butter and Cheese

For Week Ending May 30, 1925

Prices Quoted in Cents Per Pound

Creamery Butter (92 score)

	New York	Chicago	Philadelphia	Boston	San Francisco
Monday	42½	41	43½	42½	40
Tuesday	42½	41¾	43½	43	40¾
Wednesday	42	41–41½	43	42½	40¼
Thursday	42½	41½	43½	43	41
Friday	43	42	44	43½	41¼
Saturday	(1)	(1)	(1)	(1)	(1)
Average for week	42.50	41.50	43.50	42.90	40.65
Previous week	41.92	41.17	42.50	42.33	40.04
Corresponding week last year	39.60	37.80	40.60	39.80	38.15

[1] Holiday.

American Cheese (No. 1 Fresh Twins)

	New York [1]	Chicago	Boston	San Francisco [2]	Wisconsin
Monday	22½–23	22½–22¾	22 –22½	21½	21½
Tuesday	22½–23	22½–22¾	22 –22½	22	------
Wednesday	22½–23	22½–22¾	22 –22½	22	------
Thursday	22½–23	22½–22¾	22½–23	22	22½
Friday	22½–23	22½–22¾	22½–23	22	22¾
Saturday	(1)	(1)	(1)	(1)	(1)
Average for week	22.78	22.63	22.45	21.90	22.25
Previous week	21.73	21.92	21.75	20.87	21.75
Corresponding week last year	17.40	18.38	19.25	20.75	17.63

[1] Holiday. [2] Flats.

Wholesale Prices of Centralized Butter (90 Score) at Chicago

	Cents per lb.		Cents per lb.
Monday	41½	Friday	42½
Tuesday	41¾	Saturday	(1)
Wednesday	41¼		
Thursday	42	Average	41.80

[1] Holiday.

Imperial Valley Lettuce Shipments Break Record

The Imperial Valley lettuce season which ended about April 15 was notable for the increased acreage, the high percentage of inferior stock as a result of adverse weather conditions, the active market throughout most of the deal, and the new high records established for volume of shipments.

Cold weather during the early part of the deal reduced the average yield per acre and tended to make a large proportion of small-sized heads. The wind-up saw a material gain in the size of the lettuce harvested and quality of this later stock also was somewhat better. During most of the shipping period, however, quality was generally fair to ordinary. Probably not more than an average of 10% of all shipments met requirements of U. S. Grade No. 1. Nevertheless, there was an increased demand for the shipping-point inspection service conducted jointly by the Federal and State Departments of Agriculture. Many buyers demanded certified shipments.

Weather conditions delayed maturity of a considerable portion of the crop and March shipments were exceptionally heavy. Movement during that month exceeded 4,000 cars, compared with 2,600 in February, 1,750 in January, and 375 in December. Total output for the season was approximately 9,840 cars, or 300 more than the 1923–24 record. Five seasons ago only 2,890 cars of lettuce came from the Imperial Valley of California.

There was an active demand during most of the deal and cash track prices were well sustained. The f. o. b. range for January sales was $1.75–$3.50 per crate of 4 to 5 dozen heads. In February the extreme prices were $1.40 and $3.50, while March sales brought from $1.10 to $3.75 per crate. Final transactions in April were made at a range of $1–$1.45. Jobbing prices in city markets went as high as $6.50 per crate in the East but by early April had declined to $1.50–$3.50. Distribution of the Imperial Valley crop was wider and more even than ever before. Chicago took about 2,000 cars and New York more than 700 cars.

Fruits and Vegetables

Good Peach Season in Prospect

With movement of Georgia peaches rapidly increasing, the market situation for this fruit was getting attention the last week of May. Potatoes caused more excitement than any other product, when prices began to rise in the Middle West. Strawberries closed strong in most markets. Onions recovered from their recent slump, and cantaloupe and tomato prices were irregular. Combined shipments of 26 products maintained a rather steady volume of 2,100 cars per day. The week's total for new potatoes was about 2,500 cars, old potatoes 1,800, tomatoes 1,300, strawberries 1,100, and cantaloupes and oranges about 1,000 cars each.

Peaches loom as one of the most important fruits to be marketed during the five months, June to October, inclusive. The 51,700,000 bushels grown last year had an estimated farm value of $60,000,000. The peach crop usually has a value about equal to that of oranges, but ranks below grapes and apples. The total apple crop is worth more than $200,000,000 at the farm, while grapes range between $70,000,000 and $100,000,000. In the order of volume, 1924 carlot shipments of leading fruits and melons ranked as follows: Apples, 113,000 cars; oranges, 75,700; grapes, 68,500; watermelons, 45,500; peaches, 39,400; cantaloupes, 29,000; grapefruit, 19,500, and pears, 16,000 cars. Movement of peaches in carlots usually is only 30% of the total production of this fruit. California grows nearly one-fourth of all the peaches in the United States, but cans almost half of its crop and dries a considerable proportion.

Georgia is the most important peach State, with the exception of California, and last year shipped about 13,500 cars of its bumper crop of 8,342,000 bushels, or approximately 21,000 carloads. Unfavorable market conditions prevented the marketing of a large part of the production. The present season's probable shipments are estimated at 12,800 cars from a crop much lighter than that of 1924. Fruit excellent in size and quality is expected. Hileys are especially promising. Elbertas and Georgia Belles will have a relatively light crop. The season is about two weeks early on all varieties. Mayflowers began moving on May 14. These, together with shipments of other early varieties, had filled 315 cars to May 30, compared with only 25 cars from Georgia to the same time last season. Carmans are expected to start about June 10, Hileys by the 15th, and Georgia Belles and Elbertas the last week of June or early July. Mayflowers declined in New York City to a range of $2.50-$3 per six-basket carrier, and Red Birds were jobbing at $6-$7. Cincinnati quoted Uneedas at $3.25. First arrivals of North Carolina peaches sold in Washington at $3-$3.50, with top of $4 in Baltimore. Movement had started from Texas and Oklahoma, also.

The 1924 peach season was unusual in that 10,420 cars, or 77%, of Georgia's entire output rolled to market during July, compared with the customary 4,000 to 6,000 cars during that month. Supplies of cantaloupes and watermelons also were heavy, thus increasing the difficulties for Georgia growers and shippers. California's 1924 movement of fresh peaches ranked next to that of Georgia, totaling about 7,200 cars. New York shipped 3,400 cars of this fruit, and Arkansas 2,800. Other States forwarding from 1,000 to 2,000 cars each were Colorado, North Carolina, New Jersey, Utah and Illinois. The 39,400 cars from all shipping sections exceeded by 1,000 cars the highest previous record, established in 1922. Conditions on May 1, 1925, indicated only 69% of a normal crop in the southern States, as against 79% the year before, and northern producing sections suffered to some extent on account of recent cold weather.

Potatoes.—Sharp advances in potato prices featured the trading in midwestern markets and at North Central shipping points. In the East conditions were slightly unsettled but the tendency was toward higher levels. Northern stocked round whites jumped to $1.75-$2 per 100 pounds on the Chicago car-lot market, a gain of 70¢-85¢ over the opening sales of the week. F. o. b. prices were mostly around $1.50-$1.75. New York round whites ranged $1.15-$1.75 in eastern cities, with Green Mountains from Maine $1.50-$2. At Aroostook County points, bulk Green Mountains doubled the price of a week ago and closed at $1.20. Shipments of old potatoes were 400 cars lighter, totaling only 1,815, about the same as for the corresponding week last season.

Though supplies of new potatoes continued liberal, prices followed the trend of old stock. Middle-western cities quoted Alabama and Louisiana Bliss Triumphs much higher at $4.25-$4.50 sacked per 100 pounds. This variety advanced to $3.75-$4, f. o. b. Mobile, Ala. In the East, cloth-top slat barrels of South Carolina Irish Cobblers ranged $5.25-$6, touching $7 in Pittsburgh. Trading at shipping points was mostly at $5.50. Arrivals from North Carolina sold on the same level. Total output of new potatoes was 2,480 cars, of which South Carolina forwarded more than half. North Carolina came to the front with nearly 500 cars. Other new entries were Oklahoma and Arkansas. A preliminary estimate of commercial plantings in 10 second-early States was 82,700 acres, about 9,000 less than last year. New Jersey plantings are about one-fifth lighter than in 1923 and 7,000 acres below last season. Eastern Shore of Maryland and the Kearney district of Nebraska also show decreases.

Cantaloupes.—Imperial valley cantaloupes got an early start, but cool weather retarded shipments, so that total output to the end of May was actually less than to June 1, 1924. Nearly 1,000 cars came from the Valley last week, and a few from Texas, with 36 cars imported from Mexico. Supplies in city markets were rather limited and prices irregular. Compared with $8 a year ago, California Salmon Tints recently advanced in New York to $10-$11 per standard crate of 45 melons. Elsewhere these melons brought $7.50-$9, St. Louis quoting some sales as low as $6.50. The f. o. b. cash track price at El Centro declined sharply to $2, or 25¢-50¢ less than in late May, 1924. Mexican Green Meats ranged from $9.50 in New York to $5 in Minneapolis, and flat crates of poor quality stock from Texas sold at $1-$1.25 on the Kansas City market.

About June 1 last year, strawberry shipments were just reaching their peak, averaging 500 cars per day. This season, heaviest movement occurred in mid-May, with the daily average only 350 cars. Output during the week ending May 30 had dropped to 1,065 cars, or 45% less than the preceding week. As a result of the rapidly decreasing supplies, prices advanced nearly everywhere. Delaware, Maryland, and Virginia berries were jobbing mostly at 12¢-25¢, quart basis, in the East, or $4-$6 per 32-quart crate. Pittsburgh dealers got $8 on some sales. Growers in eastern Maryland received $6.75-$8 on Gandys and $3.50-$4.50 on Klondikes, while various varieties in Delaware returned $4-$7 a crate. Missouri, Kentucky, and Tennessee Aromas sold generally at $6-$6.50 in the Middle West. The berry crop in southwestern Michigan was seriously damaged by cold weather about May 17. Illinois berries also suffered from a recent freeze.

Carload Shipments of Fruits and Vegetables

Week of May 24-30, and season to May 30, with Comparisons

Product	May 24-30, 1925	May 17-23, 1925	May 25-31, 1924	Total this season to May 30	Total last season to May 31	Total last season
Apples:						
Western States	114	171	149	41,441	62,910	62,910
Eastern States	119	177	212	62,344	74,924	74,924
Asparagus	49	64	46	1,577	1,088	1,235
Cabbage	480	711	660	13,488	14,372	41,771
Cantaloupes	986	130	1,141	1,128	1,281	28,347
Cauliflower	6	16	4	4,326	4,209	4,209
Celery	172	177	110	8,072	7,240	18,104
Cherries	173	117	190	367	470	1,050
Citrus fruits, mixed	63	65	89	3,658	4,308	5,058
Cucumbers	490	315	900	2,248	1,948	7,165
Deciduous fruits, mixed	31	3	125	14	102	5,049
Eggplant	28	34	20	148	70	728
Grapefruit	243	207	387	21,039	19,328	20,031
Lemons	449	487	429	7,302	5,633	12,615
Lettuce	264	738	433	24,540	20,975	29,474
Onions	191	386	363	4,681	4,216	30,683
Oranges	941	1,077	1,455	50,045	62,686	78,361
Peaches	277	44	148	327	38	36,399
Peppers	73	35	87	726	397	2,423
Pears and prunes	38	11	3	49	38	210
Potatoes:						
Sweet	21	26	6	15,703	14,535	44,533
White—						
1924 crop	1,815	2,214	1,838	12,362	¹9,149	¹244,814
1925 crop	2,479	2,042	2,886	12,362	¹0,149	¹244,814
Strawberries	1,065	1,900	1,178	11,130	12,006	18,789
String beans	128	148	461	3,354	3,285	
Tomatoes	1,318	844	770	7,824	8,385	26,685
Vegetables, mixed	699	875	591	16,088	12,763	26,763
Watermelons	386	62	63	475	67	45,037
Total	13,075	13,036	16,955	559,400	578,695	850,092

¹ Not included in totals.

Arrivals and Prices of Fruits and Vegetables for the Week May 25-29, 1925, with Comparisons [1]

LATE POTATOES (Prices quoted on New York Round Whites, sacked per 100 pounds)

Markets	Total carlot arrivals					Prices to jobbers		
	May 25–29, 1925	May 18–23, 1925	May 27–June 2, 1924	Jan. 1–May 29, 1925	Jan. 1–June of 1924	May 25–29, 1925	May 18–23, 1925	May 25–31, 1924
New York	210	324	92	7,419	6,936	[1] $1.50–1.75	[1] $1.25–1.40	[21] $2.10–2.20
Boston	153	450	120	5,140	6,095	1.50	[1] 1.10–1.10	[2] 2.05–2.15
Philadelphia	115	98	16	2,657	2,702	1.35–1.43	1.35	1.65–1.85
Baltimore	12	23	9	771	697	1.15–1.33	1.25–1.50	2.00
Pittsburgh	53	148	82	2,287	2,040	1.65–1.75	1.15–1.25	[1] 1.75
Cincinnati	32	52	22	1,113	1,268	[1] 2.00	1.35	[1] 1.65–1.75
Chicago	219	363	149	8,182	6,792	[4] 1.75–2.00	[12] 1.05–1.15	[12] 1.45–1.60
St. Louis	42	25	27	1,325	1,482	[2] 2.00–2.10		[1] 1.60–1.70
Kansas City	54	145	47	3,327	6,075	[14] 2.00–2.25	[14] 1.35	[18] 1.50–1.75

EARLY POTATOES (Prices quoted on South Carolina Irish Cobblers, cloth-top slat barrels)

New York	410	315	468	2,205	1,832	$5.25–5.50	$5.50–5.75	$3.50–4.00
Boston	64	29	42	162	72	6.00–6.25	5.25	6.50–7.00
Philadelphia	243	132	198	1,154	795	5.50–5.75	5.25–5.50	4.25–4.75
Baltimore	78	39	71	333	224	6.00	5.50–5.75	4.00–4.50
Pittsburgh	59	62	79	365	311	6.00–7.00	5.75	5.00–5.50
Cincinnati	55	78	112	248	364	[1] 4.25	[8] 5.00–5.25	[3] 2.50–2.60
Chicago	109	155	264	924	802	[7] 4.25–4.50	[7] 2.65–2.90	[12] 2.25–2.80
St. Louis	91	84	84	544	346	[1] 4.00–4.25	[7] 3.25	[7] 2.25
Kansas City	62	76	74	387	219	[14] 4.25–4.50	[7] 3.25	[12] 2.50–2.75

TOMATOES (Prices quoted on Florida, fancy, wrapped, ripe and turning, six-basket carriers)

New York	182	235	289	2,019	2,228	$3.50–4.00	$3.50–4.00	$2.25–2.75
Philadelphia	84	77	121	847	877	2.50–3.50	2.50–3.50	3.75
Baltimore	45	55	64	508	534	3.25–3.50	2.50–4.00	4.00–4.50
Pittsburgh	31	101	60	510	367	4.00–4.25	2.50–3.00	3.75–4.00
Cincinnati	20	21	21	173	236	3.50–4.00	2.00–3.75	4.00
Chicago	86	100	107	943	939	[1] 3.25–5.50	[1] 5.50–6.00	[8] 5.50–7.00
St. Louis	36	25	27	153	164	[1] 1.50–1.75	[1] 5.00	[8] 5.00–5.50
Kansas City	27	14	31	137	197	[12] 1.25–1.50	[1] 1.75–2.00	[12] 2.00–2.25

ONIONS (Prices quoted on Texas Yellow Bermudas, standard crates)

New York	87	143	142	3,088	3,288	$1.65–1.75	$3.00–3.10	$1.65–1.75
Boston	19	28	20	848	768	3.50–3.75	3.50	1.65–1.75
Philadelphia	10	19	19	886	908	3.50	3.25–3.40	1.65
Baltimore	10	13	18	248	282	3.40–3.50	3.50	1.65–1.75
Pittsburgh	13	36	31	618	698	3.85–4.00	3.15–3.25	1.50–1.65
Cincinnati	2	10	20	169	222	3.75–4.00	1.50–2.00	1.50–1.60
Chicago	80	90	145	1,100	965	3.75–4.00	3.00–3.40	1.50–1.75
St. Louis	23	64	154	922	874	3.25	3.25	1.25–1.50
Kansas City	51	37	34	378	453	3.50	3.25	1.25–1.50

CABBAGE (Prices quoted on Virginia Wakefield, barrel crates)

New York	117	151	125	2,363	2,440	$1.50–2.00	$1.00–1.50	$1.25–1.50
Boston	31	45	28	617	672	2.75–3.00	2.00	1.50–1.75
Philadelphia	48	95	46	1,273	1,321	1.50–2.25	1.50–1.75	1.15–1.35
Baltimore	45	45	40	843	779	2.00–2.75	1.50–1.75	1.25–1.50
Pittsburgh	29	54	41	794	1,149	2.25–2.50	2.25–2.50	1.25–1.75
Cincinnati	9	27	23	397	420	[11] 1.50–2.00	2.00–2.50	[11] 1.85–2.00
Chicago	39	102	88	1,467	1,879	[11] 1.75–2.00	[11] 2.00–2.75	[11] 2.00–2.75
St. Louis	5	27	51	900	1,288	[11] 1.75–2.00	[11] 2.25	[11] 1.75–2.00
Kansas City	15	27	10	434	641	[11] 1.75–2.00	[11] 3.00–3.25	

STRAWBERRIES (Prices quoted on Virginia and Maryland Various Varieties, quart basis)

New York	215	320	386	1,907	1,774	$0.15–0.25	$0.14–0.22	$0.09–0.12
Boston	99	129	170	641	561	.16 – .30	.15 – .21	.16 – .19
Philadelphia	82	154	135	604	602	[13] 4.00–6.00	[14] 4.00–6.00	[12] 2.00–3.00
Baltimore	20	63	125	202	264	.12 – .20	.07 – .13	
Pittsburgh	53	64	86	296	353	[13] 6.00–6.50	[13] 5.50–6.00	[14] 4.50–5.00
Cincinnati	70	174	70	560	316	[13] 6.00–6.50		
Chicago	113	206	222	1,178	1,268	[13] 5.80–6.25	[13] 5.80–6.25	[14] 5.00–6.00
Kansas City	99	181	131	597	311	[13] 6.50	[13] 5.75–6.00	[14] 4.00

[1] Arrivals include all varieties of each product. Prices are the closing for the week and are for the variety or varieties specified.
[2] Maine Green Mountains.
[3] Bulk per 100 pounds.
[4] Northern Round Whites.
[5] Carlot sales.
[6] Minnesota Red River Ohios.
[7] Alabama and Louisiana Bliss Triumphs, sacked per 100 pounds.
[8] Repacked.
[9] Texas Bliss Triumphs, sacked per 100 pounds.
[10] Texas foults.
[11] Alabama and Mississippi stock.
[12] 32-quart crates.
[13] Missouri and Kentucky Aromas, 24-quart crates.
[14] Missouri and Kentucky Klondikes, 24-quart crates.

Closing Carlot Prices of Fruits and Vegetables at Shipping Points

May 25-29, 1925, with Comparisons

Product	Shipping point	Unit of sale	May 25–29, 1925	May 18–23, 1925	May 26–31, 1924
Potatoes:					
Irish Cobblers	Charleston, S. C.	Cloth-top slat barrels.	$5.50	$4.50	$3.50–4.00
Do	Afton, N. C.	Cloth-top stave barrels	5.25–5.75		
Do	Beaufort, N. C.	do	4.50–5.50		
Bliss Triumphs.	Mobile, Ala.	100-pounds sacked.	3.75–4.00	2.50–2.75	1.50–1.75
Round Whites	Waupaca, Wis	do	1.50–1.60	.95–1.00	
Do	Minneapolis and St. Paul, Minn.	do	1.60–1.75	.95–1.00	1.40–1.45
Green Mountains.	Presque Isle, Me.	100-pounds bulk.	1.20	.55– .60	
Cabbage:					
Wakefield	Norfolk, Va.	Barrel crates.	2.25–2.50	1.50	1.00–1.25
Strawberries:					
Various varieties.	Bridgeville, Del.	32-quart crates.	[1] 5.00–6.50	[1] 5.75–6.25	
Do	Selbyville, Del.	do	[1] 4.00–7.00	[1] 4.50–5.00	
Tomatoes:					
Green, wrapped, fancy.	Ocala, Fla.	6-basket carriers.	2.50	3.00	3.00–3.25
Do	Jacksonville, Texas.	4-basket carriers.	1.15–1.25		
Do	Crystal Springs, Miss.	do	1.20–1.25		
Onions:					
Yellow Bermudas.	Coachella Valley points, California.	Standard crates.	2.90–3.15	2.50–2.60	
Cantaloupes:					
Salmon Tints.	El Centro, California.	Standards 45's.	2.00		2.35–2.50
Watermelons:					
Tom Watsons.	Ocala, Fla.	Bulk per car (22–30 lb. avg.)	350–650.00		

[1] Wagonloads cash to growers.

Good Potato Season in Colorado

Colorado potato shipments had reached a total of 11,504 cars by April 11, and it seemed probable that not over 700 cars remained to be moved after that date. To a corresponding date last year, 12,820 cars were shipped and the season's total movement was 13,870 cars. The area planted in Colorado in 1923, however, was 110,000 acres, while the 1924 acreage was but 97,000. Production was placed at 11,640,000 bushels in 1924, compared with 13,530,000 the year before. Idaho and Washington each had about 1,400,000 bushels less than in 1923; in fact, the crop throughout the West was generally lighter in 1924.

On the other hand, production in the United States broke all records, so that Colorado faced the shipping season with the problem of marketing a moderate crop in competition with plentiful supplies from other sections. Fortunately, since Idaho found outlets in the Northwest and in California, Colorado did not meet as stiff competition as usual in southwestern markets, the Federal-State reporter at Denver advises.

Peak movement from Colorado occurred during the last week of September, but heaviest shipments from the whole country came the last two weeks of October. It was during this period that prices paid to Colorado growers reached lowest level of the season. Low price in the San Luis Valley, the Greeley district, and Western Slope was 55¢ per 100 pounds, but in the Valley and the Greeley district only a few sales were made at this price and 60¢ was more nearly the real bottom price. Furthermore, there were no radical fluctuations and an average to the grower considerably above the cost of production was maintained throughout the shipping season. While prices were not high, this consistent level above the cost of production is noteworthy.

Between September 15, 1924, and April 2, 1925, prices to growers in the San Luis Valley ranged from 55¢ to $1.25 sacked per 100 pounds for Brown Beautys, and from 70¢ to $1.67½ on Peachblows. Carlot shipments from the Valley totaled 4,207 cars to April 2. In the Greeley district, prices for Rurals ranged from 55¢ to $1.05 and shipments totaled 3,741 cars. More potatoes than usual were transported by truck from the Greeley district. Western Slope shipments had reached 3,473 cars by April 2, and prices on Peoples Russets ranged from 55¢ to $1.10, while Carbondale common-soil. Russet Burbanks brought from 90¢ to $1.25 during the season.

Mississippi Tomato Shipments at Height

With the movement of three cars on May 19, the 1925 Mississippi tomato season was started and a new record established for earliness of first shipments. Movement is 10 days in advance of the 1924 season. Shipments to May 30 totaled 785 cars, compared with only 6 to the same time last year, and local factors estimate 1,800 to 2,000 cars for the entire season. In 1924, the Mississippi output was 3,775 cars.

On account of low returns last year, plantings were reduced 30% to 10,800 acres. According to reports from the Federal market news representative at Crystal Springs, a long drought during the growing season was followed by rainy weather in mid-May, which gave the needed moisture for the maturity of the crop. Weather in general was favorable to the development of fine-quality tomatoes, although of smaller average size than a year ago. Yields this season may be nearly as heavy as in 1924—possibly 275–300 crates to the acre. However, sizes are smaller, as a result of the drought, and total shipments may not reach the local estimates.

At the beginning of the Mississippi shipping season, liberal supplies of Florida stock, mostly of ordinary quality and condition, depressed the markets to such an extent that they would not take Mississippi at the high opening price of $1.50–$1.75 per four-basket crate. F. o. b. prices around Crystal Springs declined rapidly to $1.10 for "wire orders," at which level the demand gradually improved. Prices later recovered to $1.20–$1.25. During the latter part of May, cool weather retarded maturity of the crop and enabled growers to pick daily only the stock necessary to be harvested. Consequently, the movement up to June 1 was somewhat lighter than it would have been had the demand been better. Peak shipments were expected about June 3, with movement continuing in moderate volume until June 15 or 20. Many of the cars are carrying Federal-State shipping-point certificates of inspection.

Michigan Potato Situation Improves

After a very dull season, with practically no sharp market fluctuations, Michigan potato growers and shippers have been heartened recently by the improved demand, as well as by the increase in prices throughout the northern producing districts since May 1.

Michigan shipments during April amounted to only 1,461 cars, compared with 2,917 in April, 1924, and 2,924 cars in April, 1923. During this period the market outlet for stock from this State was restricted practically to points in Ohio, Indiana, Kentucky, and Tennessee. The continued heavy movement from Maine and New York on the East and from Minnesota to the West, together with the severe competition from these sections, made it difficult for Michigan shippers to find a favorable outlet for their potatoes. Maine and New York stock practically eliminated Michigan potatoes from the Pittsburgh and Cleveland markets, and forced shippers to use only those markets where a preferential freight rate gave them an advantage, according to reports from the Federal-State market news representative at Grand Rapids. During April, the "carlot delivered" sales of sacked Russet Rurals on a Cadillac-rate basis ranged from 55¢ to 75¢ per 100 pounds, with most sales at 60¢–70¢. Prices to growers for bulk stock at various shipping points in Michigan were mostly 30¢–40¢, with a few points as high as 50¢. Deliveries during the entire month were very light and shipments were mostly from warehouse stocks, so that the tonnage in shippers' hands became very low by the end of April.

With the gradual cleaning up of stocks in the Western States and the decrease in heavy movement from Maine, New York, and Minnesota, as well as the relatively light early movement shipments, available market supplies decreased and demand shortly after May 1 rapidly improved. "Car lot delivered" sales on a Cadillac-rate basis advanced from 58¢–60¢ per 100 pounds on May 1 to 95¢–$1.05 by the 14th, while wagonload prices to growers had risen from a range of 30¢–40¢ to 50¢–80¢, with most sales around 60¢–70¢. There was also a gradual increase in daily shipments from Michigan. Compared with 30–50 cars per day during late April, the mid-May output was 80–100 cars a day.

As shipments from the Western States decreased, more Michigan potatoes have gone to territory usually supplied by these sections. During the early part of May, Chicago, which seldom secures much of its supply from Michigan, received original billing on 65 cars, while scattering shipments have been made daily to the St. Louis–Memphis territory, and 6 cars of table stock were billed to Sacramento and San Francisco, Calif.

The following table shows carlot movement of Michigan potatoes to April 1 and after April 1 in recent seasons:

Season	Total shipments	Shipments to Apr. 1	Shipments after Apr. 1	Percentage shipped after Apr. 1	Total crop	On hand Jan. 1
	Cars	Cars	Cars	Per cent	Bushels	Bushels
1921–22	15,237	11,579	3,658	24	27,200,000	8,160,000
1922–23	19,833	12,812	7,021	35	37,842,000	14,005,000
1923–24	20,558	13,887	6,671	32	35,796,000	13,961,000
1924–25		12,621			38,282,000	15,108,000

During the past three years, shipments from Michigan to January 1 have averaged very closely, considering the variations in total production, and during the 1922–23 and 1923–24 seasons the spring movement was very much the same. On January 1, 1925, estimated stocks on hand were over a million bushels greater than the year before. However, shipments from the State to May 16 this season were 14,982 cars, or 3,282 less than last year, with most of the loss in shipments occurring during the spring months. All factors in the State are agreed that output for the current season will not equal last year's record movement of 20,558 cars. Depending largely on market conditions and a continuation of the recently improved price levels, the most optimistic estimates of future shipments are for around 2,000 cars, probably making the total potato shipments from Michigan this season between 16,500 and 17,000 cars.

Imperial Valley Cantaloupe Season Early

The season's first car of cantaloupes from the Imperial Valley of California moved on May 7, about 10 days earlier than any previous season's first shipments. Notwithstanding the early start, subsequent shipments were considerably below the usual developments, for, up to May 21, only 82 cars by express and 19 by freight had been forwarded. The customary time for opening of the Imperial Valley season has been around May 25 in recent years.

Most of the early shipments this year were "H-B" (or Hale's Best) melons, a new variety which ripens slightly ahead of the Pollock 10–25, a leader in past seasons. Possibly not more than 10% of the total acreage was planted to this new melon. The early ripening of this variety accounted for the exceptionally early start of the season and the light shipments of the first two weeks. From past experience, it was probable that, as soon as the Pollocks began to mature, movement would increase more rapidly. Local factors predicted that output would be very light to June 1, with heavy movement between June 10 and 25. Total shipments to May 30 were 1,150 cars, compared with 1,213 to the same time last season. Weather conditions influenced the movement of the crop more than any other factor. During May, the Valley experienced a considerable amount of cool, windy weather, which caused most fields to mature slowly.

Acreage in the Imperial Valley is estimated around 30,000 this year, with a possible total crop of 5,100,000 crates. This estimate covers cantaloupes, Honey Dews, Casabas, and Persian melons; all but about 1,000 acres, however, are devoted to cantaloupes. Because of the lower average yield, the season's total shipments may not equal last year's record of 15,760 cars. In late May, a general feeling of optimism prevailed, according to reports from the Federal market news representative at El Centro. The crown set was light, an indication of limited early shipments and of fairly good prices.

This is the first year that any concerted effort was made toward advertising the Imperial Valley crop. Arrangements have been completed and an enthusiastic program is under way. Even though the cost of this advertising campaign is only nominal, amounting to around 25¢ per acre, those in close touch with it are very optimistic over the results secured so far and are predicting even greater benefits. Daily meetings of shippers are being held with the purpose of determining the best distribution of shipments.

This season an earnest attempt is being made by shippers to move only the more mature melons, as many of their difficulties in the past resulted from the practice of shipping stock too green. With general improvement in transportation conditions and the reduction of one or two days in running time to eastern markets, it was felt that the melons could be picked more nearly matured than in former years and still carry as well.

Grain

Grain Market Firm Account Crop Damage

Unfavorable crop reports with lack of moisture and claims of damage from frost, insects, and disease forced wheat futures upward, May 25–29. The cash market was firm, although receipts were more liberal. Mill takings were of slightly larger volume with the more active demand for flour but continued on a hand-to-mouth basis, while export business fell off as prices advanced and total export sales for the week were only about one-third as large as for the previous week.

Commercial stocks in the United States have been decreasing recently at the rate of about 8,000,000 bushels a week and are now about 8,000,000 bushels smaller than a year ago, although they are still larger than at this time in 1923 or 1922. Shipments from North America continue to run about 6,000,000 bushels per week but shipments from the Southern Hemisphere have decreased and world weekly shipments averaged recently about 10,000,000 bushels against about 18,000,000 bushels in February and March. Over two-thirds of the estimated surplus from the Southern Hemisphere has been exported in the twenty weeks to date.

	Wheat		Corn		Oats	
	May 25-29	May 18-23	May 25-29	May 18-23	May 25-29	May 18-23
	Bushels	Bushels	Bushels	Bushels	Bushels	Bushels
Primary receipts...	6,449,000	5,176,000	5,530,000	2,581,000	4,244,000	3,229,000
Primary receipts last year...	2,944,000	3,677,000	3,505,000	2,470,000	2,764,000	2,644,000
Primary shipments.	5,856,000	6,850,000	2,995,000	2,387,000	4,907,000	4,700,000
Primary shipments last year...	2,842,000	3,494,000	3,604,000	3,778,000	3,088,000	3,376,000
Visible supply.	34,968,000	37,173,000	17,140,000	17,383,000	35,331,000	37,349,000
Visible supply last year...	43,110,000	44,668,000	12,238,000	13,252,000	6,720,000	7,300,000
Receipts at:	Cars	Cars	Cars	Cars	Cars	Cars
Chicago.......	353	730	1,445	732	418	389
Minneapolis...	559	675	140	46	184	173
Duluth.......	1,014	1,280	....	....	75	48
St. Louis.....	418	295	449	353	345	308
Kansas City...	661	580	234	212	106	69
Omaha........	253	256	300	149	124	126
Cincinnati....	35	54	65	64	20	38
Indianapolis..	52	27	369	104	92	101
Toledo........	....	18	....	....	....	29
Milwaukee....	23	12	86	84	134	134
Wichita.......	129	113	22	90	1	1
Hutchinson..	143	115	....	3	....	....
Sioux City 1..	26	35	23	25	33	32
Cairo 1.......	....	....	....	....	....	....
Fort Worth...	72	81	35	64	47	87
Denver.......	30	20	55	42	22	16

1 Week ending Friday.

The progress of the winter wheat crop in the United States ranged from fair in most of the Ohio Valley to poor in Oklahoma and parts of Texas. Rain was badly needed in Oklahoma. The crop was beginning to ripen in Southern Kansas and was heading as far north as the Ohio Valley and southern Iowa. Spring wheat was generally doing well but growth was slow and the crop was in need of moisture in some sections.

European crop conditions according to latest reports continue generally favorable with prospects of an increase over last year's short crop. Seeding was favored by good weather in the Southern Hemisphere and an increase in wheat acreage seemed probable in Argentina.

Cash wheat at Minneapolis was unsettled, although prices closed slightly higher. Premiums were declining and the bulk of sales of No. 1 dark northern ranged 3–20¢ over the July price, against 5–25¢ last Saturday, but the July price advanced 4¢, closing at $1.64½.

Durum wheat was weak with the demand for durum flour practically at a standstill. Premiums declined and No. 1 amber durum sold at Duluth at the July price to 40¢ over.

Hard winter wheat also suffered a loss in premiums, although quotations were slightly higher. Offerings continued fairly liberal with country elevators cleaning up their stocks before harvest, while farmers were also selling more freely. The flour demand was slightly more active and mill takings increased, although mills were buying only to replace current grindings.

There were a few scattered sales of old wheat from the Southwest for export but European buyers have been practically out of the market for the new crop.

Soft red winter wheat was also firm with slight price advances, though cash prices did not follow the full upturn in futures. There was a more active milling inquiry in Cincinnati toward the close of the week but only for small lots and the flour trade at Toledo was dull. Stocks of good milling wheat at St. Louis were light. No. 2 red winter wheat was quoted Thursday at $1.93 at St. Louis, $1.92–$1.93 at Toledo and $1.94–$1.95 at Cincinnati.

CASH CORN MORE ACTIVE

The corn market was firm on account of recent frost damage, although receipts at primary markets were almost double those of the previous week. The crop suffered a severe setback by cold weather in the Middle Mississippi and Ohio Valley States and considerable damage was done in some localities, which will necessitate replanting, though much of the damaged corn will recover. Moisture was needed in most of the South.

The cash demand for corn was more active with industries buying moderately. Choice corn was wanted at Chicago by elevators, shippers, and feeders with the principal inquiry for the yellow grades. Premiums declined slightly at Minneapolis on liberal offerings and the movement to the South from Kansas City was comparatively small. Good quality white corn was wanted at Cincinnati. Country offerings were liberal but were expected to slow up with the press of field work.

The oats market showed independent strength, chiefly on account of reports of crop damage. The condition of the crop was generally fair, except in Indiana, Illinois, and Minnesota where drought and frost have been harmful. The feeding demand was of moderate volume but there was a fair export business. Elevators and cereal interests bought sparingly. Southern demand was slightly more active at Kansas City.

The barley market was firm with other grains. There was some export business and good malting barley was especially in demand. Rye was firm with fears of frost damage and need of rain in some localities. Export business was dull and milling inquiry lacking. Exports were of moderate volume but commercial stocks of this grain total over 10,000,000 bushels. Trade reports indicate that European crop prospects are favorable and that the rye crop will be materially larger this year.

Flax averaged slightly easier, although new crop futures were firm. Trade reports indicate considerable frost injury in the Northwest, but there is still time to reseed this crop. Cash flax continued in good demand and there was practically no accumulation of linseed oil. Argentine exports increased somewhat but this country still has more to ship than at this time last year.

Crimson Clover Seed Production Small

A production of crimson clover seed in Tennessee equal to that of last year, which was around 300,000 lbs., is indicated in reports to the department. The marked reduction in acreage to be cut for seed is offset by an improved condition of the crop, which promises much higher yields per acre. Weather conditions have been favorable for the setting of seed and little blight is in evidence. Low prospective prices induced many growers to plow under their crop earlier in the season. Harvesting has begun. Prices to growers have not been established.

The crimson clover seed crop in France is looking well according to latest reports. The carryover of old seed in that country is larger than usual.

Imports for the 11 months ending May 31, 1925, were 4,555,990 lbs. This is 40% less than the heavy imports of 7,576,000 lbs. during the same period ending May 31, 1924, and is slightly less than the average imports for that period. Imports for the full 12 months' period ending June 30, 1924, were 7,744,500 lbs. Recent monthly imports are below normal, only 300,700 lbs. being permitted entry during April and May. Little interest usually is manifested in this commodity until the new European crop is available, and imports are not heavy until August or September.

Present wholesale selling prices at eastern markets range $6.50–$7 per 100 lbs. compared with $8–$8.50 last year at this time, and $14–$15 in 1923. European shipments are quoted at around $6 per 100 lbs. c. i. f. Atlantic seaboard markets duty paid.

Grain Prices

Daily Weighted Price Per Bushel of Reported Cash Sales at Stated Markets, Week of May 23-29, 1925, with Comparisons of Weekly Averages

Wheat

Market and grade	Daily prices: Sat.	Mon.	Tues.	Wed.	Thur.	Fri.	Weekly averages: May 23-29, 1924	May 16-22, 1925	May 23-29, 1925
	Cents	*Cents*	*Cents*	*Cents*	*Cents*	*Cents*	*Cents*	*Cents*	*Cents*
CHICAGO									
Hd. Winter, No. 2	170	171	172	170	170	170	110	170	171
No. 3	165	167	168	168	169	165	105	160	167
Red Winter, No. 2	192	190	190	191	------	188	109	192	190
No. 3	------	------	188	------	184	------	106	------	185
MINNEAPOLIS									
Hd. Spring, No. 1	182	185	185	181	183	181	------	182	183
Dk. No. Spring, No. 1	176	179	176	176	179	179	132	176	178
No. 2	179	180	177	173	174	179	128	175	177
No. 3	182	------	168	------	176	166	124	168	175
No. Spring, No. 1	170	172	173	172	174	175	123	160	173
No. 2	168	171	174	170	172	172	121	168	172
No. 3	172	169	166	172	169	171	119	165	160
Am. Durum, No. 2	------	171	------	------	------	168	114	176	170
KANSAS CITY									
Dk. Hd. Winter, No. 2	168	174	177	172	170	174	------	167	172
No. 3	------	------	174	175	------	178	115	169	175
Hd. Winter, No. 2	162	164	167	162	168	164	108	163	164
No. 3	157	162	163	164	159	159	107	163	162
Red Winter, No. 2	170	------	------	------	------	173	108	------	171
No. 3	------	------	------	170	------	------	106	164	170
OMAHA									
Dk. Hd. Winter, No. 2	------	------	175	------	170	------	------	------	172
No. 3	------	------	------	------	------	------	------	154	------
Hd. Winter, No. 2	157	158	161	160	162	159	102	158	159
No. 3	156	157	160	158	161	158	100	159	158
ST. LOUIS									
Hd. Winter, No. 2	168	169	170	168	171	------	109	169	170
Red Winter, No. 2	187	188	190	188	193	191	114	192	188
No. 3	179	180	184	181	182	182	111	186	181
FIVE MARKETS									
All classes and grades	168	168	171	169	171	169	112	167	169
MINNEAPOLIS (cash close)									
Dk. No. Spring, No. 1	176	177	178	176	178	176	126	176	177
WINNIPEG (cash close)									
No. Spring, No. 1	188	------	195	193	198	192	105	187	193

Corn

Market and grade	Sat.	Mon.	Tues.	Wed.	Thur.	Fri.	May 23-29, 1924	May 16-22, 1925	May 23-29, 1925
CHICAGO									
White, No. 2	115	118	119	118	118	118	79	114	118
No. 3	113	115	117	116	117	117	78	113	116
Yellow, No. 2	117	119	120	119	119	120	79	117	119
No. 3	114	117	118	117	118	118	78	114	117
Mixed, No. 2	------	117	118	116	116	116	79	113	116
No. 3	112	115	116	115	115	114	76	112	115
KANSAS CITY									
White, No. 2	110	113	112	112	112	112	78	109	112
No. 3	106	------	------	110	------	111	77	108	109
Yellow, No. 2	112	115	114	114	114	113	79	111	114
No. 3	------	113	113	------	111	112	78	109	112
Mixed, No. 2	107	116	109	108	109	109	75	107	110
No. 3	------	110	108	106	------	108	74	106	108
OMAHA									
White, No. 2	108	110	------	109	110	111	75	107	110
No. 3	------	------	------	108	109	110	74	107	109
Yellow, No. 2	109	112	112	110	111	112	75	109	111
No. 3	108	111	111	109	110	111	73	108	110
Mixed, No. 2	------	109	------	108	109	109	------	106	109
No. 3	107	------	------	107	108	108	71	106	107
ST. LOUIS									
White, No. 2	116	119	118	116	117	117	81	114	117
No. 3	------	118	116	114	------	------	79	113	116
Yellow, No. 2	116	120	119	118	118	118	80	116	118
No. 3	115	119	118	117	117	117	78	114	117
Mixed, No. 2	113	118	118	------	118	116	78	113	116
No. 3	------	------	116	------	------	------	77	111	116
FIVE MARKETS									
All classes and grades	112	116	116	113	114	115	77	112	115

Oats, White

Market and grade	Daily price: Sat.	Mon.	Tues.	Wed.	Thu.	Fri.	Weekly averages: May 23-29, 1924	May 16-22, 1925	May 23-29, 1925
	Cents	*Cents*	*Cents*	*Cents*	*Cents*	*Cents*	*Cents*	*Cents*	*Cents*
CHICAGO, No. 2	47	49	48	48	49	50	48	45	48
No. 3	44	46	46	46	47	48	48	45	46
MINNEAPOLIS, No. 2	------	46	46	45	------	47	46	45	46
No. 3	42	43	43	43	44	45	45	42	44
KANSAS CITY, No. 2	48	49	50	------	50	50	51	48	49
No. 3	47	47	48	49	49	49	49	48	48
OMAHA, No. 3	45	46	46	45	46	48	47	44	46
ST. LOUIS, No. 2	49	50	49	49	50	51	50	48	49
No. 3	47	48	48	48	48	49	49	46	48
FIVE MARKETS									
All classes and grades	44	46	46	46	47	47	48	44	46

Rye

Market and grade	Sat.	Mon.	Tues.	Wed.	Thu.	Fri.	May 23-29, 1924	May 16-22, 1925	May 23-29, 1925
CHICAGO, No. 2	------	118	118	------	------	------	69	115	118
MINNEAPOLIS, No. 2	113	118	119	118	120	118	65	114	117

Barley

Market and grade	Sat.	Mon.	Tues.	Wed.	Thu.	Fri.	May 23-29, 1924	May 16-22, 1925	May 23-29, 1925
MINNEAPOLIS, No. 2	83	84	84	------	85	84	72	85	84

Flaxseed

Market and grade	Sat.	Mon.	Tues.	Wed.	Thu.	Fri.	May 23-29, 1924	May 16-22, 1925	May 23-29, 1925
MINNEAPOLIS, No. 1	282	281	281	282	279	278	241	282	281

Closing Prices of Grain Futures

Wheat

Market	July features: 1924, May 22	1924, May 29	1925, May 22	1925, May 29	September futures[1]: 1924, May 22	1924, May 29	1925, May 22	1925, May 29
	Cents	*Cents*	*Cents*	*Cents*	*Cents*	*Cents*	*Cents*	*Cents*
Chicago	107½	107¾	155¼	103½	108⅜	109	147½	160⅜
Minneapolis	113¼	114⅛	160⅛	164½	112½	113½	145⅛	154¼
Kansas City	98¾	98¾	147¾	155⅛	100	100½	140¾	152
Winnipeg	104	105⅝	176⅝	179⅛	99¾	101½	144½	150⅞
Liverpool	119½	118¾	182	186¼	118¼	117⅝	168⅞	175⅝

Corn

Market	1924, May 22	1924, May 29	1925, May 22	1925, May 29	1924, May 22	1924, May 29	1925, May 22	1925, May 29
Chicago	77	77	115⅛	118¼	76⅛	76⅝	114	118⅜
Kansas City	72⅜	72½	107⅞	110⅛	71⅞	72	108	111⅛

Oats

Market	1924, May 22	1924, May 29	1925, May 22	1925, May 29	1924, May 22	1924, May 29	1925, May 22	1925, May 29
Chicago	44⅛	44¼	45	48⅞	39¾	40	44⅜	48⅞
Winnipeg	39¾	39¾	56⅝	58⅜	38¼	38½	52⅜	54¼

[1] October futures for Winnipeg and Liverpool

Reports Favorable on Foreign Grain

Growing conditions continue favorable in Canada. Some precipitation during the week ending May 26 was reported in Alberta, and parts of Saskatchewan and Manitoba, which will be beneficial to crops stubbled in. Warmer weather is needed for good germination and plant growth. No important changes have occurred in crop conditions in Europe. Rumania reports that crops are good to average. Russian winter grain crops are now slightly above average, although not quite as good as at this time last year.

Hay

Hay Market Develops Weaker Tone

The hay market averaged slightly easier during the week ending May 29, although light receipts at some points caused local firmness. The demand was slack, with light shipments to coal mines and to the southern trade, and the moderate offerings were ample for current needs. The movement of new alfalfa increased and quotations at several markets were shifted to a new crop basis.

Pastures and meadows were benefited by showers in the upper Ohio Valley and the Atlantic Coast States and some improvement was noted in the east Gulf district. Grass lands, however, need rain in most central and eastern portions of the country and growth was slow in much of the North because of both dryness and low temperatures. Trade reports from California indicated that excessive rains had damaged grain hay and the first cutting of alfalfa, while much of the grain hay had become so matured that it would have to be cut for grain.

Receipts at—	May 25-29 1925	May 18-23 1925	May 26-31 1924	Jan. 1- May 29, 1925	Jan. 1- May 31, 1924
	Cars	Cars	Cars	Cars	Cars
Boston	72	51	72	1,886	1,709
New York	136	255	98	4,679	4,129
Philadelphia	42	61	143	1,116	1,941
Pittsburgh		75	88		3,114
Cincinnati	119	132	84	2,916	3,271
Chicago		68	188		5,207
Minneapolis-St. Paul	50	75	55	2,070	1,910
St. Louis	117	114	127	3,087	3,331
Omaha	59	51	58	2,173	2,749
Kansas City	293	303	214	11,682	11,521
Los Angeles	183	108	163	4,201	4,761
San Francisco	46	38	55	1,027	2,164

Timothy ruled easier. Receipts increased slightly at Boston, with medium and low grades continuing to make up the bulk of the arrivals. The market was draggy, with only the best cars in each grade bringing full quotations. Offerings were light at New York and surplus stocks were being reduced. The tone of the market was firm, although quotations held unchanged. Warehouse stocks at Philadelphia were large and the market was slow. Receipts of near-by hay supplied practically all the local requirements at Baltimore, while the Richmond market was practically unchanged.

The shipping trade was draggy at Cincinnati and the moderate arrivals were in excess of local needs. Interior points were reported to be underquoting this market for shipment to the South and prices worked lower. Receipts continued light at Chicago and there was a brisk demand for No. 2 hay or better.

Common and poor hay made up the bulk of the arrivals at St. Louis and met a limited demand although the light offerings of the best grades sold readily at unchanged quotations. Good timothy sold readily at Minneapolis and St. Paul.

The volume of trading at Southern markets was light with the better grades in the best demand. Quotations advanced about 50 cents at Memphis but declined at Atlanta. Only the best grades of timothy were wanted at New Orleans.

Alfalfa averaged slightly easier as the movement of the new crop increased. Alfalfa was very dull at Richmond and none was offered at Minneapolis and St. Paul. The first car of new alfalfa arrived at Omaha from Western Nebraska and was of fair quality. Prices of old crop alfalfa at this market advanced about 25 cents per ton and lighter receipts for the coming year were expected due to winter killing and insect damage. Receipts of new alfalfa increased at Kansas City and were arriving in unusually good condition. Very little old alfalfa arrived and the new crop was selling at $8-$17. The mills were buying a little but dairies and feeders were inactive while the shipping trade was very light.

No. 1 alfalfa at San Francisco held steady but increased receipts weakened the Los Angeles market and prices declined about $1. Traders were uncertain about the effect of the lowered quality due to the heavy rains. Farmers were about ready to begin the second cutting in some localities.

The prairie market was draggy. Very little feeding prairie was received at Chicago but more would have sold readily on account of the scarcity of good quality tame hay. Prairie was dull at Minneapolis and St. Paul although the limited offerings were absorbed without great pressure. Good quality prairie was slightly higher at Omaha with dry weather threatening to increase the demand for hay. The Kansas City market was quiet with only 58 cars arriving. The stockyards bought some hay and the local trade took a few cars. Very little was shipped and Kansas prairie was not quoted in New Orleans.

The straw market was firm. The demand was light at Boston but prices of rye straw advanced $1 at New York and straw was scarce and higher at Chicago.

Association Ships to Many Markets

Shipments by the Illinois Fruit Growers' Exchange, Centralia, Ill., consisted of 416 cars during the 1924 season. Total movement was made up of the following: Apples, 135 cars; potatoes, 79 cars; strawberries, 73; peaches, 65; cabbage, 47; pears, 13; blackberries, 2; raspberries and cherries, 1; green tomatoes, 1 car.

The produce was shipped to 61 markets in 17 States as follows: Illinois, 14 markets; Indiana, 7; Ohio, 7; Michigan, 6; Minnesota, 4; Mississippi, 4; Wisconsin, 3; Florida, 2; New York, 2; and to one market in each of seven other States, namely, Alabama, Kentucky, Louisiana, Missouri, Nebraska, North Dakota, and South Dakota.

The preceding season nearly 600 cars of produce were handled. These were shipped to 98 markets in 20 States.

Carload Prices of Hay and Straw per Ton at Important Markets, May 29, 1925

Commodity	Boston [1][3]	New York [1][3]	Phila-del-phia [1][3]	Pitts-burgh [1]	Rich-mond [1]	At-lanta	Balti-more	New Or-leans	Mem-phis [1]	Cin-cin-nati [1]	Chi-cago [1][2]	Min-neap-olis [1] and St. Paul	St. Louis [1]	Oma-ha [1]	Kan-sas City [1]	Los An-geles [1]	San Fran-cisco [1]	Den-ver
HAY																		
Timothy and clover:																		
No. 1 timothy	$25.00	$25.00		$21.50	$25.00	$19.75	$24.00	$23.50	$17.00		$17.00	$21.50		[4] $14.75			$20.00
No. 2 timothy	22.50	22.50	$18.50	19.00	24.00	18.75	22.00	21.50	16.00		16.00	16.50		[4] 11.50			
No. 1 light clover mixed		22.50	18.50	20.50	24.50	17.75			16.00					[4] 14.50			
No. 2 light clover mixed		19.00	16.50	19.00	23.50	16.25						14.00					
No. 1 medium clover mixed		19.00	16.50	19.50													
No. 1 clover mixed						17.25			15.00					[4] 13.00			
No. 1 clover						17.50			15.00					[4] 10.75			
Alfalfa:																		
No. 1 alfalfa		29.00		22.00	30.00		28.75	$21.00	19.00	$22.00	$22.00		$15.75	[4] 17.25	$20.50	$15.00	19.00
Standard alfalfa				20.00	28.00		26.75	20.00		[4] 20.00	[4] 20.00		[4] 15.75			14.00	
No. 2 alfalfa		25.50			25.00			19.00	16.50	[4] 16.00	[4] 16.00	18.00	10.00	[4] 13.50		12.00	
Prairie:																		
No. 1 upland						16.50				16.00	16.00	15.50	11.00	10.75			
No. 2 upland										15.00	15.00	12.00	9.00	8.25			
No. 1 midland										13.00	13.00		10.25				
STRAW																		
No. 1 wheat			15.25	12.00		15.25			10.50	7.50	7.50						
No. 1 oat		14.50	14.25	$13.50		15.75			10.00	8.00	8.00						
No. 1 rye		18.50	15.25	20.50		18.75			14.00	8.50	8.50						

[1] Hay quotations represent average of cash sales at these markets. [2] Hay quotations based on U. S. grades. [3] Large bales. [4] Nominal. [5] New crop.

▭ ▱   *Feed*   ▱ ▭

Feed Markets Turn Easier

Receding prices were the rule in the feed markets during the week May 25-30 with wheat feeds for future shipment showing the greatest loss. A combination of larger production by flour mills, particularly in the Southwest, and a contraction in the demand from the mixing and jobbing trade brought about the decline in wheat feeds. The declines in other commercial feeds were only slight as the small consuming demand was offset by light offerings.

The fact that prices are at an exceptionally high level for this season of the year naturally made for cautious buying, with most of the trade limiting their purchases to single carlots or split cars for spot needs. On the other hand, few jobbers were found willing to sell the future market short, their main deterrent being the recent firmer tendency in oats. The pastures and haylands situation is being carefully watched by these operators as an important indication of the feed price trend during the summer months.

Production of the wheat feeds as stated showed further improvement while the demand eased. Oil meal stocks and production were good but the export demand readily absorbed surplus offerings, the latter factor being the principal price sustaining influence. An unusually light interest was shown in these high protein feeds by domestic feeders, evidently the result of satisfactory pasture conditions and an unwillingness to feed the more expensive products.

Stocks, generally, were fair and the movement good.

Wheat mill feeds.—Wheat mill feed offerings increased and prices showed an easier tendency. The demand was easier but restricted to near-by stuff or split cars. Bran for equal shipment July, August, and September sold at $23 per ton in Kansas City, or $5 per ton under prompt. Bids were reported from that market for more of these positions on the same basis. The demand for middlings and shorts was even less than that for bran, with the result that the heavier offal narrowed its premium over bran. Production of the southwestern mills was larger than last week but the output of northwestern mills was about unchanged. Buffalo mills offered some feed for June shipment but the speculative demand in eastern markets was practically nil. In fact, both the Philadelphia and Boston markets withdrew their support to a certain extent, claiming that present transit lake and rail supplies moving to the East are more than ample to take care of near-by demand in the eastern territory. A bid of $24 for June bran, or $3 less than prompt, was reported in the Minneapolis market from Boston, but this was practically the only indication received from distributing markets as to their ideas on future prices. The light speculative interest in the market evidences that the majority of the trade are expecting lower prices, yet there has not been any great pressure to sell, the only feed being that which is delivered by mills to jobbers on contract. Mills generally are operating at low capacity and appear content to await developments, as old contracts and the present mixed car trade will take care of their production for some time. Heavy feeds were only a shade lower. Twenty-day shipment June middlings brought $29 in Minneapolis and small lots of June middlings $28.50. Flour middlings were available in that market at $33 and red dog at $40-$41.50, depending on quality. Stocks and the movement were fair.

Cottonseed cake and meal.—Stocks of cottonseed cake and meal at the mills were larger than at the same time last year. Extreme quiet prevailed in the demand for these feeds both for spot and transit and deferred offerings. The latter offerings were in liberal supply from the South. Transit and spot stocks were fully ample to meet the demand but did not prove burdensome as little is placed in transit unsold at present. Some inquiries were reported for export, but these were mostly for deferred shipment. Prices held fairly firm with shipments after June quoted 25-50 cents per ton over June. The hull trade was very dull with stocks at mills heavy and prices lower.

Linseed cake and meal.—As a result of the very light domestic demand the market on linseed cake and meal was easier with resellers frequently offering discounts of $1 from mill prices in order to dispose of their holdings. In the East prices were relatively higher than in the Northwest, $43.75 being asked for 34 per cent meal in Buffalo while $41 was asked in Minneapolis. The export situation continues to be a very important factor. Several of the Minneapolis mills are now using Canadian flax and, figuring the drawback allowed on cake made from imported flax, that market is now close to an export basis. In fact, some export sales were recently made but they figured only a little more than $40, the basis for domestic fine meal in sacks. Production was good and resulted in some accumulation. Summer shipment meal was quoted nominally at $40 Minneapolis, at which figure several bids were received.

Gluten feed.—There was very little change in the gluten feed situation, except that shipments by the mills seemed to be heavier. Prices in most markets were only nominal, merely representing the views of the trade as to what possibly could be realized for a few cars. Asked prices in eastern markets for a few cars running were around $40-$41 per ton bulk basis.

Hominy feed.—Despite the strong corn markets the demand for hominy feed was very poor. Offerings both by mills and resellers were very liberal at slightly lower prices than last week. Resellers seemed inclined to press the market and quoted in some instances $1.50 per ton less than was asked by the mills. Yellow hominy feed was scarce and sold at the same price as white and in a few cases slightly higher. Production, stocks, and the movement were good.

Alfalfa meal.—In the alfalfa meal market buyers took hold in a limited way, merely to meet their immediate needs. New alfalfa hay is now moving to the markets quite freely, hence mixers are inclined to hold off their buying of meal until new crop offerings can be secured at substantial discounts from present prices. However, the trade generally believes that the switch from the old to the new crop will require at least 30 days. Spot stocks were light especially the choice grade, and held at firm prices. Colorado mills were reported as having closed down and as disposing of their old crop stocks.

Carload Prices of Feedstuffs at Important Markets, May 29, 1925

[Per ton, bagged, sight-draft basis]

Commodity	Boston	Phila-delphia	Balti-more	At-lanta	Mem-phis	Cincin-nati	Buf-falo	Chi-cago	Minne-apolis	St. Louis	Oma-ha	Kan-sas City	Los An-geles	San Fran-cisco
Wheat bran:														
Spr n	$35.50	$34.50	$34.50	$38.00			$31.00	$30.50	$27.00					
Soft winter		38.00	37.00	38.50	$32.00	$34.50	33.00					$28.00		$44.00
Hard winter		35.50		38.00	31.00	34.00	32.50			$30.00	$27.50	28.00	$37.00	
Wheat middlings:														
Spring (standard)	37.00	36.50	36.50	42.00		36.00	33.00	33.00	30.00					
Soft winter	41.25	41.00		43.00		39.00	30.00					44.00		36.00
Hard winter				42.00		39.00	38.00			35.00	34.50	34.00		
Hard winter wheat shorts (brown)	36.25	35.75		41.00	36.50		38.00				32.50	32.50	45.00	
Wheat millrun				40.00					32.00			30.00	40.00	43.00
Rye middlings							31.50		28.00					
High protein meals:														
Linseed	49.00	48.25	48.25				46.50	44.50	45.50	41.00	45.00	46.50	43.00	45.00
Cottonseed (43%)	49.50	48.50	48.25		40.50	43.50	47.00	46.00	46.00	43.50		42.00		51.00
Cottonseed (41%)	47.50	45.50	46.00		38.50	42.50	45.00	48.00	44.00	41.00		40.00		
Cottonseed (36%)	45.00	44.25	44.00	36.00	35.50	40.50	42.50	41.00	41.50	38.00				
Digester feeding tankage (60%)									50.00	50.00	50.00	50.00	50.00	
No. 1 alfalfa meal (medium)				31.00	28.00		29.00	28.00				26.00	22.50	29.00	24.00
Linseed	43.70	42.90	39.70			35.70	41.20	32.90	35.00					
White hominy feed	44.50	43.50	45.00	44.00		40.00	42.00	42.50		41.50				
Yellow hominy feed			45.00	44.00		40.00	42.50	41.00		41.50				
Ground barley						42.00		39.50				41.00	39.00	
Dried beet pulp		38.00											41.00	37.00

¹ Nominal.   ² Rolled.

Cotton

Prices Decline

Cotton prices fluctuated within a narrow range during the period May 25–29. On May 30 almost all the markets were closed in observance of Memorial Day. The narrowness of the markets was largely attributed to the waiting attitude of the trade for the issuance by the crop reporting board of the department on June 2 of the report of the condition of the crop as of May 25. Trade estimates of the condition appeared to be centered around 75.

Activity in the spot cotton departments of the trade was reported as dull with sales very limited. Final prices on May 29 were down about ½¢ per lb. for both spots and futures.

On the New York Cotton Exchange July future contracts closed at 22.98¢ as compared with 23.20¢ last week and 29.65¢ one year ago, and on the New Orleans Cotton Exchange July future contracts closed at 23.30¢ as compared with 23.49¢ last week. July future contracts on the Chicago Board of Trade declined 15 points during the week, closing at 23.50¢.

The average price of No. 5 or Middling cotton in 10 designated spot markets was down 21 points, closing at 23.83¢ as compared with 30.58¢ one year ago.

Spot sales for the week amounted to 11,140 bales as compared with 18,020 bales the previous week and 16,536 bales for the corresponding period in 1924.

Reports indicated sizable freight engagements for cotton to be shipped shortly out of the New York certificated stock, which now amounts to about 135,000 bales as compared with about 195,000 bales in March.

Closing Future Prices on the Future Exchanges

May 29, 1925, with Comparisons

Month	New York					New Orleans				
	May 29, 1925	May 29, 1924	June 2, 1923	June 3, 1922	May 29, 1921	May 29, 1925	May 29, 1924	June 2, 1923	June 3, 1922	June 3, 1921
	Cts.	Cts.	Cts.	Cts.	Cts.	Cts.	Cts.	Cts.	Cts.	Cts.
July	22.98	29.65	23.90	20.63	12.96	23.30	29.61	26.14	20.50	12.50
October	22.47	26.45	24.22	20.41	13.70	22.56	26.72	25.48	20.00	13.25
December	22.67	25.73	22.92	20.25	14.10	22.18	25.90	22.90	19.75	13.62
January	22.25	25.56	22.60	20.15	14.17	22.19	25.38	22.25	19.61	13.74
March	22.50	25.60	22.55	19.97	14.47	22.32	25.30	22.15	19.34	14.01

Daily Closing Quotations for No. 5 or Middling Spot Cotton at 10 Designated Spot Markets, Week of May 25–30, 1925, with Comparisons

Market	May 25–30, 1925						May 26–31, 1924					
	Mon.	Tue.	Wed.	Thu.	Fri.	Sat.	Mon.	Tue.	Wed.	Thu.	Fri.	Sat.
	Cts.	Cts.	Cts.	Cts.	Cts.	Cts.	Cts.	Cts.	Cts.	Cts.	Cts.	Cts.
Norfolk	24.50	24.30	24.25	24.25	24.00	(¹)	31.00	30.48	30.00	30.25	(¹)	(¹)
Augusta	24.25	24.43	24.24	24.00	24.00	(¹)	30.75	30.63	30.31	30.25	30.25	(¹)
Savannah	24.00	23.93	23.72	23.77	23.75	(¹)	30.75	30.56	30.56	30.50	30.70	30.95
Montgomery	24.20	24.20	24.24	24.00	24.00	(¹)	30.00	29.88	29.75	29.75	29.75	30.00
New Orleans	24.00	24.00	23.93	23.94	24.05	(¹)	31.19	30.75	30.75	30.88	30.31	30
Memphis	23.50	23.50	23.50	23.25	23.25	(¹)	31.50	31.50	31.25	31.25	31.25	31.50
Little Rock	24.12	24.12	24.00	24.00	24.00	(¹)	31.00	30.75	30.50	30.50	30.50	30.50
Dallas	23.55	23.60	23.40	23.40	23.40	(¹)	30.60	30.40	30.30	30.30	30	(¹)
Houston	23.95	23.93	23.73	23.72	23.75	(¹)	31.25	31.31	31.00	31.00	31.00	31.25
Galveston	24.13	24.15	23.95	23.95	23.95	(¹)	31.40	31.25	31.16	31.31	31.00	31.45
Total	24.02	24.04	23.85	23.85	23.83		30.94	30.75	30.54	30.58	30.74	30.99

¹ Holiday.

Stocks of Egyptian cotton at Alexandria, Egypt, on May 29, were reported to be 198,000 bales of approximately 750 lbs. gross weight, compared with 149,000 bales on May 30, 1924. Stocks of Indian cotton at Bombay, India, on May 29, were reported to be 898,000 bales of approximately 400 lbs. gross weight, compared with 841,000 bales on May 30, 1924.

Receipts at 10 Designated Spot Markets, August 1, 1924–May 29, 1925, and Stocks on May 29, 1925, with Comparisons

[Compiled from commercial reports]

Market	Aug. 1, 1922–June 1, 1923	Aug. 1, 1923–May 30, 1924	Aug. 1, 1924–May 29, 1925	5-year average Aug. 1–May 30, 1920–1924	June 1, 1923	May 30, 1924	May 29, 1925	5-year average May 30, 1920–1924
	1,000 bales	1,000 bales	1,000 bales	1,000 bales	1,000 bales	1,000 bales	1,000 bales	1,000 bales
Norfolk	258	404	383	321	43	33	44	62
Augusta	287	189	230	344	21	19	27	72
Savannah	414	395	615	666	25	27	17	77
Montgomery	60	51	82	56	8	8	6	14
New Orleans	1,319	1,284	1,852	1,255	97	137	115	230
Memphis	1,081	898	1,276	971	69	47	24	170
Little Rock	170	112	170	170	19	6	4	33
Dallas	84	124	196	114	3	3	3	11
Houston	2,658	3,445	4,713	2,662	45	78	150	163
Galveston	2,287	2,799	3,604	2,449	61	71	167	161
Total	8,628	9,701	13,168	9,009	391	419	557	1,013

Cotton Movement August 1, 1924–May 29, 1925, and Stocks May 29, 1925, with Comparisons

[Compiled from commercial reports]

	Aug. 1, 1913–May 29, 1914	Aug. 1, 1920–May 27, 1921	Aug. 1, 1921–June 2, 1922	Aug. 1, 1922–June 1, 1923	Aug. 1, 1923–May 30, 1924	Aug. 1, 1924–May 29, 1925	5-year average Aug. 1–May 30, 1920–1924	Per cent this year is of 5-year average
	1,000 bales	1,000 bales	1,000 bales	1,000 bales	1,000 bales	1,000 bales	1,000 bales	Per cent
Port receipts	10,249	5,748	5,607	5,523	5,422	8,952	5,964	150.1
Port stocks	514	1,577	857	363	363	543	849	64.0
Interior receipts	7,268	6,815	6,807	7,128	7,120	10,040	6,918	145.1
Interior stocks	295	1,497	215	447	356	341	816	41.8
Into sight	14,226	9,978	9,519	10,781	11,015	14,435	10,508	137.4
Northern spinners' takings	2,542	1,695	1,989	2,197	1,704	1,830	2,044	89.5
Southern spinners' takings	2,915	2,456	3,518	4,081	3,673	4,043	3,357	120.4
World's visible supply of American cotton	2,790	4,512	3,001	1,432	1,541	2,253	2,898	77.7

Exports of American Cotton

August 1, 1924, to May 29, 1925, with Comparisons

[Compiled from Government and commercial reports]

To—	Aug. 1, 1913–May 29, 1914	Aug. 1, 1921–June 2, 1922	Aug. 1, 1922–June 1, 1923	Aug. 1, 1923–May 30, 1924	Aug. 1, 1924–May 29, 1925	4-year average Aug. 1–May 30, 1921–1924	Per cent this year is of 4-year average
	Bales	Bales	Bales	Bales	Bales	Bales	Per cent
Great Britain	3,931, 989	1,525, 065	1,239, 763	1,607, 907	2, 474, 251	1, 460, 874	169.4
France	1,067, 794	680, 398	587, 149	672, 607	857, 723	607, 186	141.3
Germany	2,749, 447	1, 297, 309	845, 015	1, 192, 554	1, 802, 935	1, 084, 741	166.2
Italy	449, 453	396, 435	444, 100	491, 988	639, 971	437, 338	150.9
Japan	337, 844	727, 789	555, 885	544, 192	805, 117	561, 062	143.5
China	2, 978	82, 919	16, 824	27, 650	36, 365	39, 152	92.9
Spain	268, 607	270, 527	270, 837	192, 035	290, 734	223, 328	112.7
Belgium	180, 186	152, 249	161, 147	158, 261	218, 491	162, 318	134.6
Canada¹	133, 221	155, 267	176, 492	131, 140	171, 997	145, 094	118.1
Other countries	236, 290	177, 601	203, 308	221, 718	475, 005	228, 127	208.2
Total	8, 724, 019	5, 435, 559	4, 442, 367	5, 340, 052	7, 752, 609	4, 952, 221	156.5

¹ Exports to Canada are for the period Aug. 1 to Apr. 30.
² Includes 49,357 bales to Russia.
³ Includes 180,086 bales to Russia.

Exports for the week ending May 29 amounted to 50,537 bales, compared with 85,940 bales the previous week, 55,029 bales for the corresponding week in 1924, and 92,722 bales for the week ending May 29, 1914.

Stocks of American Cotton at European Ports

[Compiled from commercial reports]

At—	May 29, 1914	May 30, 1919	May 28, 1920	May 27, 1921	June 2, 1922	June 1, 1923	May 30, 1924	May 29, 1925	5-year average [1]
	1,000 bales	*1,000 bales*	*1,000 bales*	*1,000 bales*	*1,000 bales*	*1,000 bales*	*1,000 bales*	*1,000 bales*	*1,000 bales*
Liverpool	812	334	889	619	403	277	316	576	519
Manchester	59	47	109	76	40	34	58	108	75
Continent	837	284	532	480	500	215	273	483	400
Total	1,708	665	1,500	1,175	1,033	526	647	1,167	994

[1] 1920-1924.

Cottonseed Price Quotations

Week of May 18-23, 1925, with Comparisons

City	May 18-23, 1925		May 19-24, 1924		May 20-25, 1923	
	Car lot	Wagon lot	Car lot	Wagon lot	Car lot	Wagon lot
	Per ton	*Per ton*	*Per ton*	*Per ton*	*Per ton*	*Per ton*
Charlotte, N. C.	$40	$35	$40	$30-35		
Raleigh, N. C.	40	38			$40	$40
Atlanta, Ga.	43.50					
Augusta, Ga.	40					
Little Rock, Ark.	38-40	35			45	40
Fort Smith, Ark.		30				
Greenwood, Miss.	42	37				
Guthrie, Okla.	34					
Memphis, Tenn.	40	37			50	48
Dallas, Tex.	[1] 42					
Houston, Tex.	[1] 40					

[1] Nominal.

Premium Staple Cotton

A good demand for premium staple cotton was reported at New Orleans with premiums unchanged. There were a few sales reported at Memphis with offerings light.

Some of the sales reported at these two markets during the period, May 25-29, were:

	Cents
New Orleans:	
No. 5 or Middling to No. 4 or Strict Middling, full 1⅛ to 1 3/16 ins.	29.50
No. 5 or Middling, 1⅛ ins.	29.00
No. 4 or Strict Middling, 1 1/16 ins.	27.50
Memphis:	
No. 5 or Middling to No. 4 or Strict Middling, 1 1/16 ins.	27.50

Average Premiums for Staple Lengths of the Grade No. 5 or Middling, May 29, 1925, with Comparisons

	New Orleans			Memphis		
	May 29, 1925	May 31, 1924	June 2, 1923	May 29, 1925	May 31, 1924	June 2, 1923
No. 5 short staple	*Cents* 24.05	*Cents* 31.30	*Cents* 27.50	*Cents* 23.50	*Cents* 31.50	*Cents* 27.50
Length in inches:	*Points*	*Points*	*Points*	*Points*	*Points*	*Points*
1 1/16	250	100	50	[1] 250	[1] Even.	Even.
1⅛	550	175	100	[1] 600	[1] 50	100
1 3/16	800	275	150	[1] 1,050	[1] 100	150
1¼	1,150	400	225	[1] 1,450	[1] 150	350
1 5/16		500	300			
1⅜		600	400			

[1] Nominal.

Spot Cotton Quotations for May 29, 1925, and Sales During Week of May 25-29, 1925

Price of No. 5 or Middling spot cotton for May 29, the commercial differences in price between No. 5 and other grades of American Upland cotton at each of the 10 markets named, and average differences and prices for the corresponding day in previous years, together with the total number of bales sold during the week of May 25-29, 1925, in each of the markets and total for all the markets, with comparisons, as reported by the cotton exchanges

Grade	Norfolk	Augusta	Savannah	Montgomery	Memphis	Little Rock	Dallas	Houston	Galveston	New Orleans	Average: May 30, 1925	May 31, 1924	June 2, 1923	June 2, 1922	June 4, 1921	May 28, 1920	May 29, 1919
White Standards:	*On* [1]	*On*	*On*	*On*	*On*	*On*	*On*	*On*	*On*	*On*	*On*	*On*	*On*	*On*	*On*	*On*	*On*
No. 1 or Middling Fair	100	100	100	88	100	125	90	100	100	110	101	192	92	181	240	375	214
No. 2 or Strict Good Middling	75	75	75	63	75	100	75	75	80	80	77	157	69	140	190	303	163
No. 3 or Good Middling	50	50	50	38	50	75	63	50	65	60	55	123	48	96	128	238	113
No. 4 or Strict Middling	25	38	38	25	25	40	38	35	40	35	34	83	26	56	63	125	60
No. 5 or Middling	24.00	24.00	23.75	24.00	23.50	24.00	23.40	23.65	23.95	24.05	23.83	30.99	27.04	20.51	11.32	40.60	31.94
	Off [1]	*Off*	*Off*	*Off*	*Off*	*Off*	*Off*	*Off*	*Off*	*Off*	*Off*	*Off*	*Off*	*Off*	*Off*	*Off*	*Off*
No. 6 or Strict Low Middling	63	75	63	63	50	50	63	60	60	50	60	101	27	56	110	290	158
No. 7 or Low Middling	163	150	150	140	100	125	160	150	150	140	143	230	66	133	230	768	428
No. 8 or Strict Good Ordinary [2]	250	250	250	240	200	250	275	275	275	250	252	365	116	223	335	1,115	723
No. 9 or Good Ordinary [2]	350	350	350	340	300	375	400	400	400	350	362	490	170	315	438	1,393	958
Spotted:	*On*		*On*			*On*			*On*	*On*	*On*	*On*					
No. 3 or Good Middling	25	Even	25	Even	Even	25	Even	Even	20	25	12	42					
	Off		*Off*			*Off*			*Off*	*Off*	*Off*	*Off*					
No. 4 or Strict Middling	Even	13	Even	25	25	25	25	35	35	Even	18	8					
No. 5 or Middling	63	50	75	63	50	50	63	60	75	60	61	94					
No. 6 or Strict Low Middling [2]	163	138	150	138	100	100	160	150	175	150	142	204					
No. 7 or Low Middling [2]	250	238	250	213	150	200	300	275	800	250	243	325					
Yellow Tinged:	*On*	*On*	*On*	*On*		*On*					*On*	*On*					
No. 2 or Strict Good Middling	25	25	13	13	25	25	15	25	20	Even	2	19					
	Off	*Off*	*Off*	*Off*		*Off*					*Off*	*Off*		*On*			
No. 3 or Good Middling	Even	25	25	25	50	25	50	50	50	40	34	27	Even	5	50	203	173
No. 4 or Strict Middling	75	75	75	75	75	50	90	100	100	80	80	74	38	*Off* 61	143	335	264
No. 5 or Middling [2]	175	150	150	150	100	150	125	150	150	175	148	173	93	163	248	500	418
No. 6 or Strict Low Middling [2]	288	250	250	250	150	200	250	275	275	250	244	290	138	240	370	730	613
No. 7 or Low Middling [2]	375	375	375	350	200	300	375	400	400	375	353	412	188	325	470	1,000	890
Light Yellow Stained:																	
No. 3 or Good Middling	75	75	75	75	50	100	125	100	100	100	88	87					
No. 4 or Strict Middling [2]	125	150	150	150	75	150	150	150	150	150	140	143					
No. 5 or Middling [2]	250	225	225	225	100	200	210	225	225	225	211	215					
Yellow Stained:																	
No. 3 or Good Middling	150	150	150	150	150	150	165	200	190	150	161	140	66	130	218	460	413
No. 4 or Strict Middling [2]	225	200	200	200	175	200	190	250	240	225	211	198	124	223	310	638	563
No. 5 or Middling [2]	325	300	300	275	200	250	250	325	325	300	285	275	171	310	418	790	705
Gray:																	
No. 3 or Good Middling	37	50	35	38	150	40	40	25	25	45	49	34					
No. 4 or Strict Middling [2]	100	75	85	88	175	75	75	60	75	75	88	84					
No. 5 or Middling [2]	150	138	150	138	200	125	125	100	150	125	140	146					
Blue Stained:																	
No. 3 or Good Middling [2]	125	138	125	125	250	125	175	125	125	125	144	128	95	155	268	585	553
No. 4 or Strict Middling [2]	175	150	175	175	275	150	200	175	200	175	185	174	133	233	363	723	663
No. 5 or Middling [2]	275	250	250	250	300	225	275	250	300	275	265	261	173	310	460	870	785
Sales for week, bales	314	843	110	58	175	55	158	2,081	3,330	4,016	[3] 11,140	[3] 16,536	[3] 10,397	[3] 39,435	[3] 63,159	[3] 23,554	[3] 134,919

[1] The differences are stated in terms of points or hundredths of a cent per pound. By "On" is meant that the stated number of points is to be added to the price of No. 5 and by "Off" is meant that the stated number of points is to be subtracted from the price of No. 5.

[2] These grades are not tenderable on future contracts made subject to section 5 of the United States cotton futures act, as amended, on the future exchanges at New York, New Orleans, and Chicago.

[3] Total sales. Sales from Aug. 1, 1924, to May 29, 1925, amounted to 4,778,807 bales, compared with 3,753,544 bales during the corresponding period in 1924 and 3,459,769 bales in 1923.

Foreign Crops and Markets

Wheat Situation in the Danube Basin

Early estimates for 1925 indicate a very slight reduction in the area planted to winter wheat and rye in the Danubian countries, including Czechoslovakia, Austria, Hungary Yugoslavia, Bulgaria, and Rumania, according to G. C. Haas, American agricultural commissioner at Vienna. Crop conditions are reported as being generally favorable. It is as yet too early to forecast the probable yield, but the outlook is for good crops. All price reports in that area are based upon reviews of the American price situation, and foreign market prices exert greater influence in the Danube Basin than they did formerly. Comparative prices in Vienna for January, 1925, showed American wheat selling at $2.19 per bushel, against $2.04 for domestic wheat. By April the price for American wheat in Vienna had fallen to $1.83 against $1.95 for Austrian grain.

That stocks of wheat and wheat flour through the Danube Basin are low seems to be borne out not only by the imports, but also by the fact that the lack of capital and high interest rates prohibit the holding of wheat any length of time. Notwithstanding high transportation costs, North and South American wheat are being imported into Austria, Yugoslavia, and Rumania at prices which are on a competing basis with domestic wheat when differences in quality are considered.

The American agricultural commissioner at Vienna reports the comparative average monthly prices of domestic and imported American wheat in the Vienna market from January to April, 1925, as follows:

Month	Domestic wheat	American New York wheat
	Cents per bushel	Cents per bushel
January	203.8	219.3
February	217.2	217.9
March	214.3	204.2
April	195.2	183.0

Austria: Prices of American Wheat Delivered in Vienna Compared with New York Prices for the Same Dates, December 28, 1924, to April 11, 1925

[Converted to cents per bushel at current New York exchange rates]

Dates	New York prices	Freight at Trieste	Transport to Vienna and other expenses	Total cost at Vienna
	Cents per bushel	Cents per bushel	Cents per bushel	Cents per bushel
Dec. 25-Jan. 3	189.0	8.4	12.9	210.3
Jan. 4-10	192.0	8.7	12.9	213.6
Jan. 11-17	199.0	8.4	12.6	220.0
Jan. 18-24	204.8	7.8	12.6	225.2
Jan. 25-31	214.4	7.2	12.6	234.2
Feb. 1-7	206.6	7.2	12.7	226.5
Feb. 8-14	197.2	6.9	12.6	216.8
Feb. 15-21	199.0	7.2	12.5	218.7
Feb. 22-28	206.4	6.6	12.3	225.3
Mar. 1-7	204.8	6.0	12.3	223.0
Mar. 8-14	190.6	6.0	12.5	209.1
Mar. 15-21	177.8	6.9	12.5	197.1
Mar. 22-28	178.5	7.8	12.5	198.8
Mar. 29-Apr. 4	163.1	9.0	12.6	184.7
Apr. 5-11	164.8	9.0	12.6	180.4

Rumania to Import Wheat

One of the significant features of the foreign wheat situation at present is the fact that Rumania is placing orders for Argentine and American wheat and Egyptian flour. The 1924 crop in Rumania amounted to only 74,000,000 bushels as against 102,000,000 bushels in 1923. Before the war Rumania was an important competitor of the United States in European wheat markets. In spite of the additions to her pre-war territory, Rumania has not been able to produce an exportable surplus of consequence since the war.

The position in which Rumania finds herself at present seems to be due primarily to land reform and the failure of the country

thus far to adjust its agriculture to new conditions. The tendency of the peasant landholders is to produce only for their own needs. This has led to an increase in the area planted to corn, since the Rumanians use more corn than other cereals in their diet. Corn is also better suited than wheat to intensive cultivation on small areas.

While the stocks of wheat in Rumania are low, stocks of corn are high. Stocks of corn have accumulated notwithstanding the fact that there are no regulations against exports. The reason for the accumulation seems to be high export duties and high transportation charges. Export duties in Rumania are so much higher than in Yugoslavia that Rumania has been unable to compete with corn from that source. The recent law permitting certain firms to import wheat, likewise gave these firms the right to export corn without paying the export duty.

Colonial Wool Prices Show Heavy Decline

The third series of colonial wool sales for 1925, which opened in London on May 5, closed on May 14 with a decline in values of from 15 to 25 per cent compared with closing rates of the second series held in March, according to Mr. E. A. Foley, the American agricultural commissioner at London, England. The quantity to be offered was originally given as 135,000 bales, but owing to the heavy fall in values registered at the opening of the series owners decided to curtail offering to 68,886 bales. The series therefore occupied eight selling days with an average daily offering of 8,500 bales.

Out of the quantity offered only 43,000 bales were sold, the British taking 18,000 bales, mostly crossbreds, the Continent 24,000 bales, practically all of which consisted of merinos, and the United States 1,000 bales, leaving about 115,000 bales to be carried forward to the next series. The better tone noticeable at the end of the second series in March led dealers to believe that at that time that the bottom had been reached in wool prices. While the situation in the interval from March to the opening of the third series indicated that this early opinion would not prove to be the case, sellers were not prepared for the slump which actually took place. Quotations on merinos at the opening of the third series were 15 to 20 per cent lower. In crossbreds, greasy offerings opened at an average fall of 30 per cent. Scoureds and slipes at the opening were quoted 25 per cent lower. As soon as it was evident that the trade would not absorb the quantity available for the series it was decided to curtail the program. At the same time it was announced that no further sales would be held in Australia before July 1. After this there was a much better demand and prices improved all around.

Closing quotations, however, were still considerably below the closing rates of the second series. As compared with last series' closing rates the following decreases took place. Australian and New Zealand greasy merinos 10 to 20 per cent lower; scoured merinos 10 to 15 per cent lower. Australian greasy crossbreds, 20 to 25 per cent lower; scoured crossbreds 20 per cent lower. New Zealand greasy crossbreds 20 to 25 per cent lower; scoured 20 per cent lower and slipes 15 to 25 per cent lower.

Mediterranean Almond Crop is Below Average

On the basis of current reports, the Mediterranean Basin will have less than average quantities of almonds to export this season, according to E. A. Foley, American agricultural commissioner at London, and various consular officers in the producing regions. Total imports of almonds, shelled and unshelled, into the United States since 1920 have averaged about 26,000,000 pounds annually, only a fraction of which comes from regions other than the Mediterranean Basin. Foreign exporters of almonds are reticent about discussing future prices, but indications are that quotations this autumn will be higher than they were last season.

Reports agree that the damage was particularly severe in southern France and Morocco. In France the carry-over of stocks from the 1924 crop are small. The American and English demand was very heavy all last winter. As this demand was principally for shelled almonds, local firms have been shelling even their soft shelled and semisoft-shelled varieties. It is believed that present supplies are insufficient to tide over the summer, and prices have risen phenomenally.

It is possible that the Sicilian crop will be slightly below average, although some reliable reports indicate an average crop. The general outlook in Spain is excellent, and the crop of the Balearic Islands promises to be approximately normal.

CPSIA information can be obtained
at www.ICGtesting.com
Printed in the USA
BVHW031156021118
531990BV00020B/1574/P